stitch wear play

stitch wear play

20 CHARMING PATTERNS FOR **BOYS & GIRLS**

Mariko Nakamura

INTERWEAVE™
interweave.com

Contents

Introduction

I started designing clothes when I was 10 years old, in a kind of game played with my mother, Akiko. I would show her drawings of my designs, we would go shopping together and choose fabrics, and then she would sew my designs into actual garments for me. I have especially warm memories from that time, particularly of my aunt Fumiko, to whom I owe a large part of my love for craft and design. Growing up in the company of such talented women was an inspiration and a privilege.

I continued to design clothes throughout my teenage years, and in time I learned the skills needed to make them up myself rather than having to rely on my mother to sew for me. I went on to study fashion design at the Bunka Fashion College in Tokyo, Japan, and after I graduated, I worked for four years within the fashion industry in Japan before moving to Britain.

I started making children's clothes after I became a mother of two. I envisaged simple, easy-to-make and easy-to-wear garments that my children would be comfortable in, and that I could make special by using vintage fabrics, buttons and ribbons found in flea markets and thrift stores. I wanted to create wardrobe staples that were easy to mix and match with other garments to create various looks for different occasions.

This book contains some of the garments that I have designed over the last couple of years, garments that my children have particularly liked wearing. All the shapes are loose-fitting so movement isn't restricted, and I have chosen practical fabrics that can be laundered time and time again. Many of the pieces can be worn with others in the collection, or layered or combined with purchased pieces. There are two sections, Spring–Summer and Fall–Winter, both containing garments for boys and for girls.

While these are not projects for complete sewing novices, they are not complicated to make: you need to be competent with a sewing machine and able to do a couple of basic hand stitches, but none of the garments uses couture techniques or much hand-sewing. There are paper patterns in four sizes for each garment (see page 142 for sizing information), and detailed instructions accompany step-by-step drawings to take you through every stage of sewing your own garments.

I do hope you enjoy making some of these clothes as much as I have enjoyed designing and making them, and that your children love the results as much as mine do.

MARIKO NAKAMURA

spring–summer

CHOOSE CRISP COTTONS AND CLASSIC LINEN TO MAKE
A SERIES OF GARMENTS SUITABLE FOR ALL ASPECTS
OF SPRING AND SUMMER, FROM A BEACH OUTFIT TO A
LONG-SLEEVED DRESS FOR COVERING UP IN THE SUN,
OR A PRACTICAL BUT GOOD-LOOKING SHIRT.

Suntop and shorts

AS BOTH PIECES CAN BE WORN AS SEPARATES, THIS IS A VERSATILE VACATION OUTFIT: PATTERN INSTRUCTIONS ARE ON PAGE 50. TRY THE SUNTOP WITH THE SIDE-BUTTON SKIRT, PAGES 22 AND 78, OR THE SHORTS WITH THE GIRL'S SHIRT, PAGES 18 AND 70. TURN TO PAGES 32 AND 100 FOR THE SHIRRED HEADBAND.

Tunic with bow

PRETTY AND COMFORTABLE, THIS TUNIC LOOKS
GOOD WITH TROUSERS OR OVER A SKIRT: PATTERN
INSTRUCTIONS ARE ON PAGE 56. IT CAN ALSO BE
LAYERED OVER A T-SHIRT OR COTTON SHIRT. THE TUNIC
IS SHOWN HERE WITH THE GIRL'S SHORTS WITH BOWS,
PAGES 28 AND 90.

Striped dress

AN EASY-TO-MAKE, EASY-TO-WEAR,
LOOSE-FITTING SUNDRESS THAT CAN BE
LAYERED OVER A LONG-SLEEVED T-SHIRT
FOR COOLER EVENINGS: PATTERN
INSTRUCTIONS ARE ON PAGE 62.

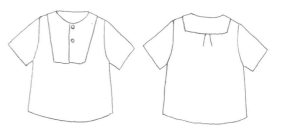

Boy's shirt

THIS PRACTICAL, PULL-ON SUMMER SHIRT LOOKS GOOD IN PLAIN
AND PRINTED FABRICS, OR YOU CAN USE TWO FABRICS TO CREATE
A CONTRAST YOKE: PATTERN INSTRUCTIONS ARE ON PAGE 66. THE
SHIRT IS SHOWN HERE WITH THE BOY'S SHORTS, PAGES 20 AND 74.
TURN TO PAGE 18 FOR THE GIRL'S SHIRT.

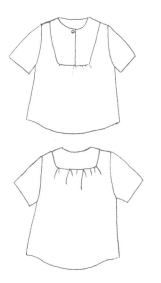

Girl's shirt

THIS VERSION OF THE BOY'S SHIRT ON PAGE 16 HAS SOFT GATHERS RATHER THAN A CRISP BOX PLEAT: PATTERN INSTRUCTIONS ARE ON PAGE 70. THE SIMPLE-TO-STITCH EMBROIDERY ON THE FRONT YOKE IS OPTIONAL: SEE PAGE 141 FOR INSTRUCTIONS.

Boy's shorts

A RELAXED FIT AND A DRAWSTRING WAIST PLUS PATCH POCKETS MAKE
THESE SHORTS PRACTICAL AS WELL AS GOOD-LOOKING: PATTERN
INSTRUCTIONS ARE ON PAGE 74. THE SHORTS ARE SHOWN HERE WITH
THE BOY'S LINEN SHIRT, PAGES 26 AND 86.

Side-button skirt

THIS SKIRT HAS A SIDE OPENING THAT BUTTONS UP, PLUS A DRAWSTRING WAIST FOR A GOOD FIT: PATTERN INSTRUCTIONS ARE ON PAGE 78. THE SKIRT IS SHOWN HERE WITH THE GIRL'S SHIRT, PAGES 18 AND 70.

Linen dress

WITH A DROPPED WAISTLINE AND DOUBLE-
BREASTED FRONT, THIS DRESS HAS A
NAUTICAL AIR—PERFECT FOR SEASIDE
VACATIONS: PATTERN INSTRUCTIONS ARE
ON PAGE 82. THIS IS ANOTHER VERSATILE
GARMENT THAT CAN BE LAYERED OVER A
T-SHIRT, OR WORN UNDER A CARDIGAN.

Boy's linen shirt

THE LINEN DRESS ON PAGE 24 HAS BEEN
INTERPRETED AS A SHIRT FOR A BOY,
RETAINING THE SAME NAUTICAL AIR:
PATTERN INSTRUCTIONS ARE ON PAGE
86. THE SHIRT IS SHOWN HERE WITH THE
BOY'S SHORTS, PAGES 20 AND 74.

Girl's shorts with bows

THESE CUTE SHORTS HAVE BEEN MADE WITH A CONTRAST LINING ON THE BOWS AND WAISTBAND, BUT YOU COULD MAKE THEM IN JUST ONE FABRIC: PATTERN INSTRUCTIONS ARE ON PAGE 90. THE SHORTS ARE SHOWN LEFT WITH THE TUNIC WITH BOW, PAGES 12 AND 56.

Box-pleated dress

A FLOWING, LONG-SLEEVED DRESS THAT WORKS AS A COVER-UP IN THE SUN AS WELL AS BEING PERFECT FOR COOLER EVENINGS: PATTERN INSTRUCTIONS ARE ON PAGE 94. THE DRESS SHOWN HERE IS MADE IN COTTON FABRIC, BUT LINEN WORKS BEAUTIFULLY, OR THIN JERSEY FOR A FALL VERSION.

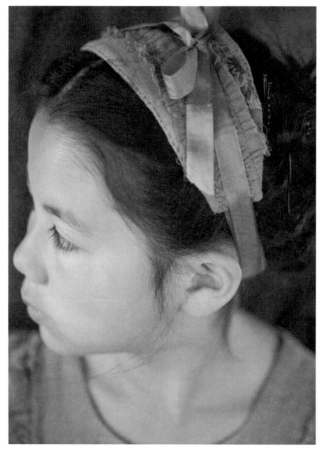

Shirred headband

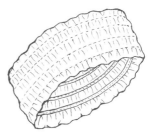

A SWEET AND VERY PRACTICAL HEADBAND FOR KEEPING HAIR OUT OF THE WAY ON THE BEACH: PATTERN INSTRUCTIONS ARE ON PAGE 100. THIS VERSION MATCHES THE SUNTOP AND SHORTS, PAGES 10 AND 50.

Layered headband

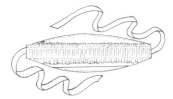

A PERFECT WAY OF USING UP SMALL SCRAPS OF LOVELY FABRICS LEFT OVER FROM OTHER PROJECTS: PATTERN INSTRUCTIONS ARE ON PAGE 102.

fall-winter

FALL NEEDS VERSATILE GARMENTS THAT CAN BE
LAYERED OVER VESTS AND LONG-SLEEVED SHIRTS
ON CHILLY DAYS. FOR WINTER, CHOOSE WARM WOOL
FABRICS AND MAKE STAPLE ITEMS THAT WILL GET
LOTS OF WEAR.

Unisex jacket

A LOOSE-FITTING JACKET THAT'S IDEAL FOR BOYS AND GIRLS ALIKE—JUST CHANGE THE PLACEMENT OF THE BUTTONS: PATTERN INSTRUCTIONS ARE ON PAGE 104.

Jersey dress

THE IDEAL LAYERING DRESS, THIS CAN BE WORN OVER
A COTTON TOP, A FINE-KNIT SWEATER OR A LONG-
SLEEVED T-SHIRT, DEPENDING ON THE WEATHER: PATTERN
INSTRUCTIONS ARE ON PAGE 110.

Skirt with bow

THIS ELASTIC-WAISTED SKIRT IS EASY AND
COMFORTABLE TO WEAR, AND THE CONTRAST PANEL
AND LONG-TAILED BOW ADD STYLISH TOUCHES:
PATTERN INSTRUCTIONS ARE ON PAGE 114.

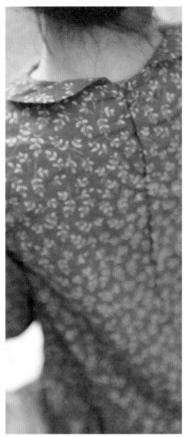

Round-collared dress

THIS DRESS WILL BECOME A STAPLE GARMENT IN A GIRL'S
FALL AND WINTER WARDROBE: PATTERN INSTRUCTIONS ARE
ON PAGE 118. IT'S LOOSE-FITTING ENOUGH TO BE WORN OVER
A T-SHIRT FOR EXTRA WARMTH, AND CAN BE MADE IN ANY
LIGHTWEIGHT FABRIC.

Puff-sleeved dress

WITH ITS PRETTY PUFFED SLEEVES AND
TIERED SKIRT, THIS IS A PERFECT PARTY
DRESS: PATTERN INSTRUCTIONS ARE
ON PAGE 124. THIS VERSION IS MADE IN
JERSEY FABRIC, BUT COTTON OR SILK
WOULD LOOK GOOD, TOO.

Boy's raglan jacket

THIS JACKET IS AN EASY SHAPE FOR AN ACTIVE BOY TO WEAR: PATTERN INSTRUCTIONS ARE ON PAGE 130. THIS VERSION IS MADE IN LIGHTWEIGHT BUT WARM WOOL; CORDUROY OR HEAVY LINEN WOULD ALSO WORK WELL.

Instructions

ON THE FOLLOWING PAGES YOU WILL FIND LISTS OF
MATERIALS, STEP-BY-STEP DRAWINGS AND DETAILED
INSTRUCTIONS ON HOW TO MAKE UP ALL OF THE PROJECTS
IN THIS BOOK. THERE ARE ALSO FABRIC LAYOUTS TO HELP
YOU EFFICIENTLY CUT OUT THE PATTERN PIECES.

Suntop and shorts

FABRIC

Lightweight printed cotton, 53¼ x 36¾:39½:42:45¼"
(135 x 93:100:107:115 cm)

OTHER MATERIALS

Lightweight fusible interfacing, 8¼:8¾:9:9½ x 4¾"
(21:22:23:24 x 12 cm)

Elastic ⅜" (1 cm) wide, 19:19¾:20½:21¼"
(48:50:52:54 cm)

Sewing thread to match fabric

TECHNIQUES

Gathering (page 139).

PATTERN PIECES

See pattern sheets E and F.

All pieces cut on straight grain unless otherwise specified.

Seam allowances are ⅜" (1 cm) unless otherwise stated.

Sample is size 3 (see page 142).

PATTERN PIECES IN BOOK POCKET

1 Front yoke: cut 1 on the fold from fabric

2 Back yoke: cut 1 on the fold from fabric

3 Front yoke facing: cut 1 on the fold from fabric
   + 1 interfacing

4 Back yoke facing: cut 1 on the fold from fabric
   + 1 interfacing

5 Front suntop: cut 1 on the fold from fabric

6 Back suntop: cut 1 on the fold from fabric

7 Front shorts: cut 2 from fabric

8 Back shorts: cut 2 from fabric

PATTERN PIECES TO BE MEASURED OUT

9 Suntop ruffle: 20½:21¼:22:23 x 3½:4:4¼:4¾"
   (52:54:56:58 x 9:10:11:12 cm), cut 2 from fabric

10 Suntop shoulder ties: 1⅛ x 35½:35¾:36¼:36¾"
   (3 x 90:91:92:93 cm), cut 2 on the bias on the fold
   from fabric

11 Shorts waistband: 26:27½:29:30¾ x 2"
   (66:70:74:78 x 5 cm), cut 1 from fabric

FABRIC LAYOUT

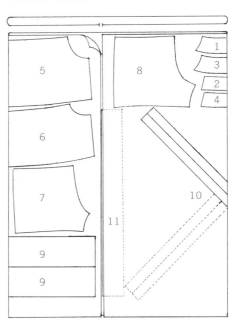

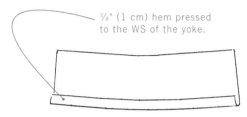

³⁄₈" (1 cm) hem pressed
to the WS of the yoke.

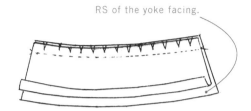

RS of the yoke facing.

SUNTOP

1 Press under ³⁄₈" (1 cm) along the lower edge of each yoke. Iron the interfacing pieces onto the wrong side of the yoke facings.

2 Right sides together, sew the front yoke to the front yoke facing along the top edge. Neaten the seam allowances, turn the pieces right side out, and press the seam.

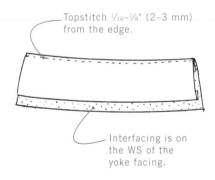

Topstitch ¹⁄₁₆–¹⁄₈" (2–3 mm) from the edge.

Interfacing is on the WS of the yoke facing.

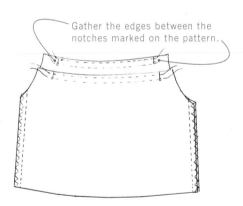

Gather the edges between the notches marked on the pattern.

3 Topstitch the top edge. Repeat Steps 1–3 with the back yoke and yoke facing.

4 Right sides together, sew the front and back suntop together at the side seams. Neaten the seam allowances and press them toward the back. Gather (see page 139 for technique) both the front and back suntop between the notches on the top edges and pull the gathers up so that each edge matches the length of the appropriate yoke.

RS of the yoke.

RS of the suntop.

5 Pin the right side of the front yoke facing to the wrong side of the gathered top edge of the front suntop. Sew the seam and press the seam allowances toward the yoke. Repeat to sew the back yoke facing to the back suntop.

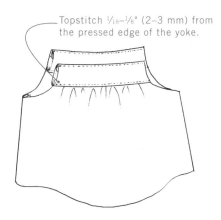

Topstitch 1/16–1/8" (2–3 mm) from the pressed edge of the yoke.

6 Pin the pressed-under edge of the yoke over the seam allowances and topstitch it in place on the right side.

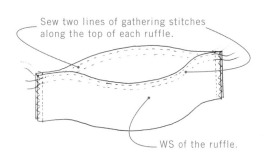

Sew two lines of gathering stitches along the top of each ruffle.

WS of the ruffle.

7 Sew the ruffles right sides together at the short ends. Neaten the seam allowances and press them toward the back. Gather (see page 139 for technique) the top edge of the ruffle and pull the gathers up so that the edge matches the lower edge of the suntop.

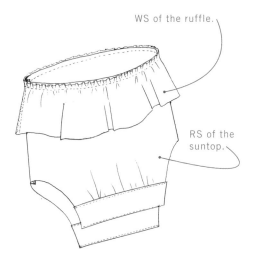

WS of the ruffle.

RS of the suntop.

8 Right sides together, sew the gathered edge of the ruffle to the lower edge of the suntop. Neaten the seam allowances and press them toward the suntop, then topstitch them in place.

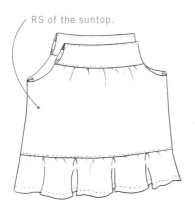

RS of the suntop.

9 Press under and sew a double ⅜" (1 cm) hem all around the bottom edge of the ruffle.

10 Fold and press a shoulder tie in half along its length. Open the tie flat again and press each raw edge to the middle. Then fold and press it in half again. On the armhole, match the side seam with the middle point of one tie and pin the folded edges over the raw edge of the armhole. Fold in ⅜" (1 cm) at each short end, then sew the open edges together along the length of the tie, binding the armhole and creating the shoulder tie in one step. Repeat with the other tie on the other armhole.

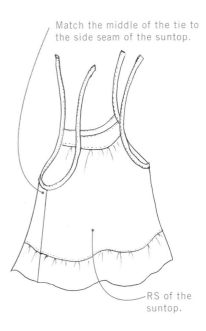

Match the middle of the tie to the side seam of the suntop.

RS of the suntop.

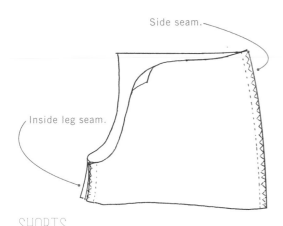

Side seam.

Inside leg seam.

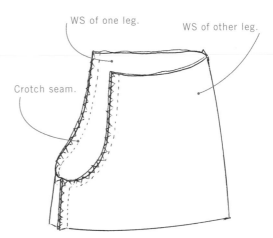

WS of one leg.

WS of other leg.

Crotch seam.

SHORTS

1 Right sides together, sew one front and one back shorts leg together along the inside leg and the side seams. Neaten all seam allowances and press them toward the back. Repeat with the other front and back legs.

2 Turn one leg right side out and slip it inside the other leg, matching all seams and raw edges. Right sides together, sew the crotch seam and neaten the seam allowances.

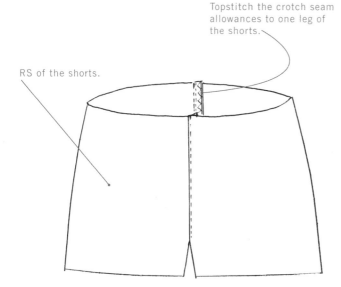

Topstitch the crotch seam allowances to one leg of the shorts.

RS of the shorts.

3 Turn the shorts right side out. Press the crotch seam allowances to one side and topstitch them in place.

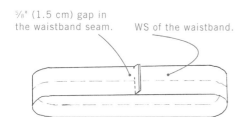

⅝" (1.5 cm) gap in the waistband seam.

WS of the waistband.

4 Press the waistband in half along its length. Right side in, sew the short ends together, leaving a ⅝" (1.5 cm) gap toward the lower edge, as shown.

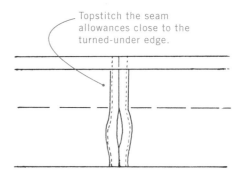

Topstitch the seam allowances close to the turned-under edge.

5 Press the seam allowances open, then turn under and topstitch them. Press under a ⅜" (1 cm) hem around the upper edge of the waistband.

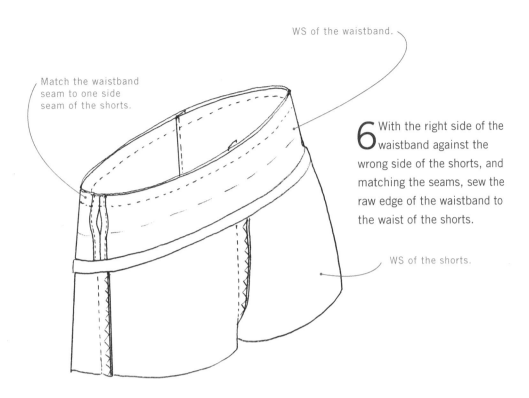

Match the waistband seam to one side seam of the shorts.

WS of the waistband.

6 With the right side of the waistband against the wrong side of the shorts, and matching the seams, sew the raw edge of the waistband to the waist of the shorts.

WS of the shorts.

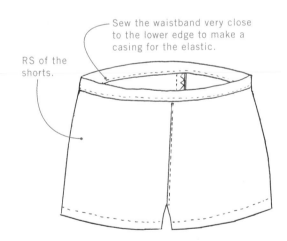

Sew the waistband very close to the lower edge to make a casing for the elastic.

RS of the shorts.

7 Fold the waistband in half to the right side and sew it in place. Press under and sew a double ³⁄₈" (1 cm) hem around the bottom of each leg.

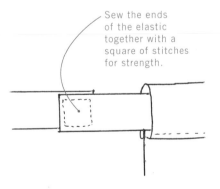

Sew the ends of the elastic together with a square of stitches for strength.

8 Thread the elastic through the gap in the waistband and around the casing. Adjust it to fit, overlap the ends and sew them together.

Tunic with bow

FABRIC

Double gauze cotton, 61 x 21¾:23¼:24½:26¾"
  (155 x 55:59:62:68 cm)

OTHER MATERIALS

Cotton tape 2" (5 cm) wide, 39½" (100 cm)
Bias binding ¾" (2 cm) wide, 36¼:39:39¾:41¼"
  (92:99:101:105 cm)
Sewing thread to match fabric

TECHNIQUES

Gathering (page 139).
Binding a center back opening (page 136).
Binding an armhole (page 135).

PATTERN PIECES

See pattern sheet E.
All pieces cut on straight grain unless otherwise specified.
Seam allowances are ⅜" (1 cm) unless otherwise stated.
Sample is size 3 (see page 142).

PATTERN PIECES IN BOOK POCKET

1 Front: cut 1 on the fold
2 Back: cut 1 on the fold
3 Front yoke: cut 1 on the fold
4 Back yoke: cut 2
5 Front yoke facing: cut 1 on the fold

6 Back yoke facing: cut 2
7 Shoulder ruffle: cut 2

PATTERN PIECES TO BE MEASURED OUT

8 Hem ruffle: 25¼:26¾:28½:30 x 5:5½:6:6¼"
  (64:68:72:76 x 13:14:15:16 cm), cut 2 on the fold

FABRIC LAYOUT

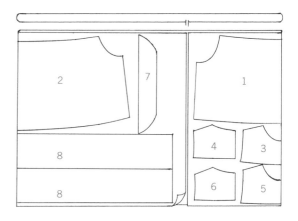

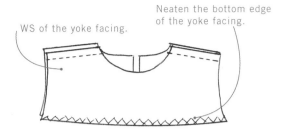

WS of the yoke facing.

Neaten the bottom edge of the yoke facing.

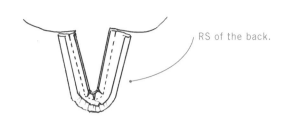

RS of the back.

1 Right sides together, sew the front and back yoke facings together at the shoulder seams. Press the seam allowances open and neaten the lower edges of both pieces. Repeat with the front and back yokes, though you do not need to neaten the lower edges.

2 Cut open the back as marked on the pattern to make the center back opening. Using bias binding, bind the opening (see page 136 for technique).

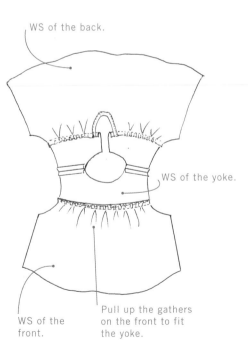

WS of the back.

WS of the yoke.

WS of the front.

Pull up the gathers on the front to fit the yoke.

3 Gather (see page 139 for technique) the top edges of the front and back between the notches marked on the pattern piece. On the front, pull up the gathers so the piece fits the lower edge of the front yoke. On each side of the center back opening, pull up the gathers to make the edges ⅜" (1 cm) shorter than the lower edges of the back yokes. Right sides together, pin the gathered edge of each piece to the lower edge of the appropriate yoke, arranging the back as shown. Sew the seams and press the seam allowances upward.

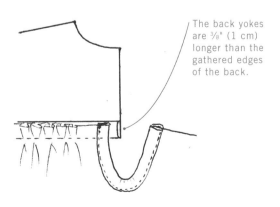

The back yokes are ⅜" (1 cm) longer than the gathered edges of the back.

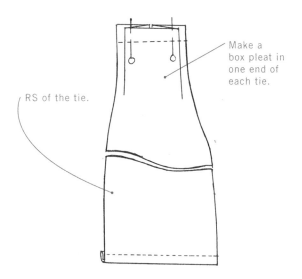

RS of the tie.

Make a box pleat in one end of each tie.

4 Cut the cotton tape in half to make two ties. Pleat one end of each tie as shown (see page 137 for technique) and stitch across, ¼" (0.7 cm) from the end. Turn under and sew a double ³⁄₁₆" (0.5 cm) hem on the other end of each tie.

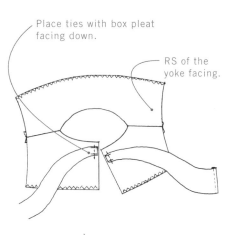

Place ties with box pleat facing down.

RS of the yoke facing.

5 Place a tie on the right side of each edge of the center back of the yoke facing, as marked on the pattern. Sew them in place ⁵⁄₁₆" (0.8 cm) from the center back edge.

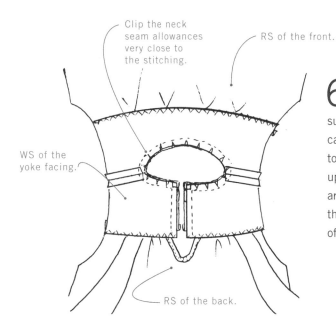

Clip the neck seam allowances very close to the stitching.

RS of the front.

WS of the yoke facing.

RS of the back.

6 Right sides together, pin the yoke facing to the yoke, matching the neck edges. Make sure that the free ends of the ties do not get caught in the pinning or stitching. From the top of the bound center back opening, sew up the center back of one side of the yokes, around the neck, then down the other side of the center back to the top of the other side of the bound opening. Clip all curves.

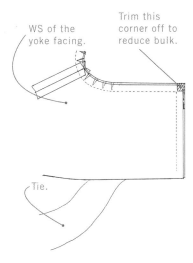

WS of the yoke facing.

Trim this corner off to reduce bulk.

Tie.

7 Trim away the corner of the center back above each tie, as shown, to reduce bulk.

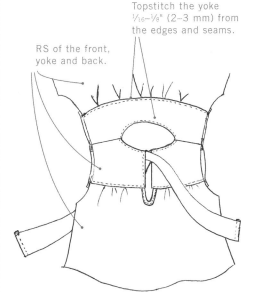

RS of the front, yoke and back.

Topstitch the yoke ⅟₁₆–⅛" (2–3 mm) from the edges and seams.

8 Neaten the neck seam allowances then turn the yoke facing to the inside. Push the corners out neatly and press, making sure the layers are flat and aligned. Topstitch along the lower edges of the yoke and up the center back opening and around the neck, as shown.

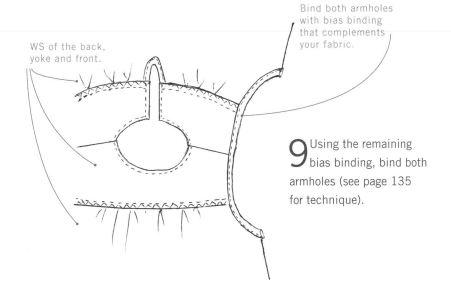

WS of the back, yoke and front.

Bind both armholes with bias binding that complements your fabric.

9 Using the remaining bias binding, bind both armholes (see page 135 for technique).

10 Sew two lines of stitching along the straight edge of each shoulder ruffle to finish the edge. Sew the first line ³⁄₁₆" (0.5 cm) from the edge and the second ⅛" (3 mm) from the edge. Sew gathering stitches (see page 139 for technique) along the curved edge.

The gathering stitches start and end at these points.

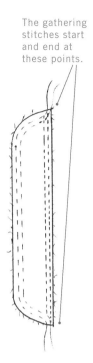

RS of the ruffle. RS of the tunic.

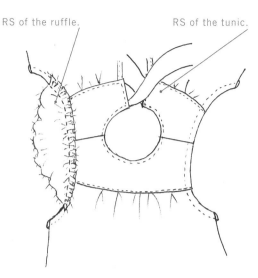

11 Pull up the gathers to fit between the notches on the armholes. With the wrong side of the ruffle against the right side of the yoke (so that the raw edges are visible on the right side), pin the gathered edge of each ruffle to the edge of the appropriate armhole, covering the binding. Topstitch the ruffles in place, sewing ³⁄₁₆" (0.5 cm) from the edge of the ruffle.

WS of the tunic.

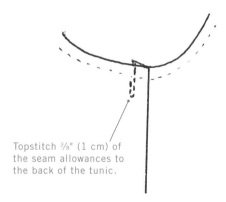

Topstitch ⅜" (1 cm) of the seam allowances to the back of the tunic.

12 Right sides together, sew the front and back together at the side seams. Neaten the seam allowances and press them toward the back. Topstitch ⅜" (1 cm) of each seam below the armhole to keep the seam allowances in place.

13 Right sides together, sew the hem ruffles together at the short ends. Neaten the seam allowances and press them toward the back. Sew a straight line of stitching along the lower edge, ³⁄₁₆" (0.5 cm) from the edge. Gather (see page 139 for technique) the top edge of the ruffle and pull the gathers up so that the edge matches the lower edge of the tunic.

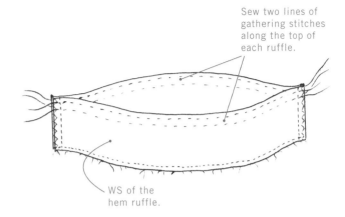

Sew two lines of gathering stitches along the top of each ruffle.

WS of the hem ruffle.

WS of the hem ruffle.

RS of the tunic.

14 Right sides together, pin the gathered edge of the ruffle to the lower edge of the tunic. Sew the seam, neaten the seam allowances, and press them toward the tunic, then topstitch them in place.

Striped dress

FABRIC

Lightweight linen or cotton striped fabric,
  64½ x 25¼:27½:29½:32" (164 x 64:70:75:81 cm)

OTHER MATERIALS

Lightweight fusible interfacing, 10¼ x 11" (26 x 28 cm)

Cotton tape 2" (5 cm) wide, 39½" (100 cm)

Bias binding ¾" (2 cm) wide, 30¼:32:33½:35"
  (77:81:85:89 cm)

Sewing thread to match fabric

TECHNIQUES

Binding an armhole (page 135).

Binding a center back opening (page 136).

Attaching facings (page 138).

Gathering (page 139).

PATTERN PIECES

See pattern sheet A.

All pieces cut on straight grain unless otherwise specified.

Seam allowances are ⅜" (1 cm) unless otherwise stated.

Sample is size 3 (see page 142).

Front bodice and front neck facing patterns are given as
  half-width, but should be traced off to produce full-
  width patterns to follow fabric layout shown.

The front and back neck facings are shared with the Jersey
  Dress (see page 110) and the Puff-Sleeved Dress (see
  page 124). The back bodice is shared with the Jersey Dress.

PATTERN PIECES IN BOOK POCKET

1 Front bodice: cut 1 from fabric

2 Back bodice: cut 1 on the fold from fabric

3 Side bodice: cut 2 from fabric

4 Front neck facing: cut 1 on the fold from fabric
  + 1 interfacing

5 Back neck facing: cut 2 from fabric + 2 interfacing

PATTERN PIECES TO BE MEASURED OUT

6 Skirt: 25½:26¾:28:29 x 13⅝:14¾:16:17⅛"
  (65:68:71:74 x 34.5:37.5:40.5:43.5 cm),
  cut 2 on the fold from fabric

FABRIC LAYOUT

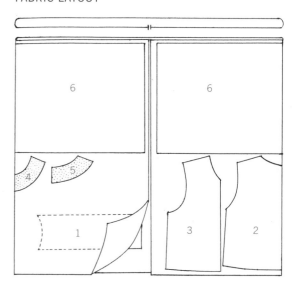

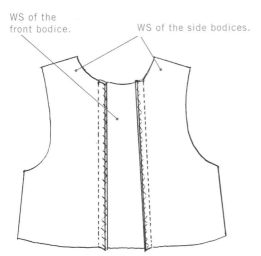

WS of the
front bodice.

WS of the side bodices.

1 Right sides together, sew the front bodice to the side bodices along the front seams. Finish the seam allowances and press them toward the bodice front, then topstitch them to hold them flat.

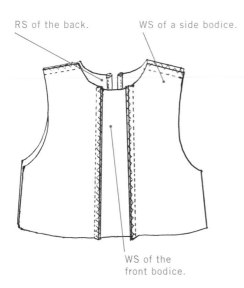

RS of the back.

WS of a side bodice.

WS of the
front bodice.

3 Right sides together, sew the front and back together at the shoulder seams. Finish the seam allowances and press them toward the back.

2 Using bias binding, bind the center back opening (see page 136 for technique).

Bind the center back opening with bias binding that complements your fabric.

RS of the
back bodice.

4 Using the remaining bias binding, bind the armholes. (see page 135 for technique).

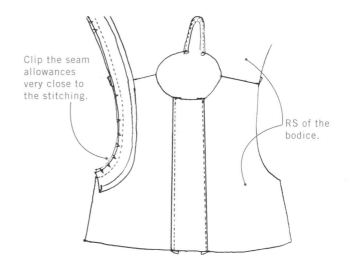

Clip the seam allowances very close to the stitching.

RS of the
bodice.

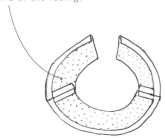

Interfacing is the on
WS of the facing.

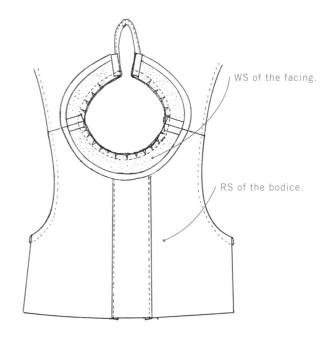

WS of the facing.

RS of the bodice.

5 Iron the interfacing pieces onto the wrong side of all the neck facings. Sew the shoulder seams and press them open. Turn under and press ⅜" (1 cm) along the lower edge of the facing.

6 Right sides together, pin the neck facing to the bodice neck. Press under each short end of the facing to align with the center back opening. Sew the facing in place (see page 138 for technique), but do not sew across the short straight ends.

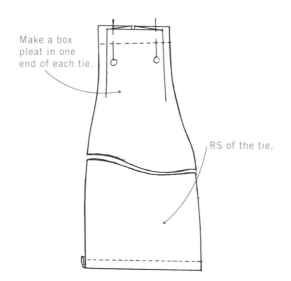

Make a box
pleat in one
end of each tie.

RS of the tie.

7 Cut the cotton tape in half to make two 19¾" (50 cm) ties. Pleat one end of each tie as shown (see page 137 for technique), press then sew across the folds, ³⁄₁₆" (0.5 cm) from the end.

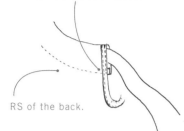

The topstitching across the short ends of the facing holds the ties in place.

RS of the back.

8 Slip the pleated end of a tie into each open short end of the facing. Topstitch across the short ends and lower edge of the facing, sewing the ties in place as you do so.

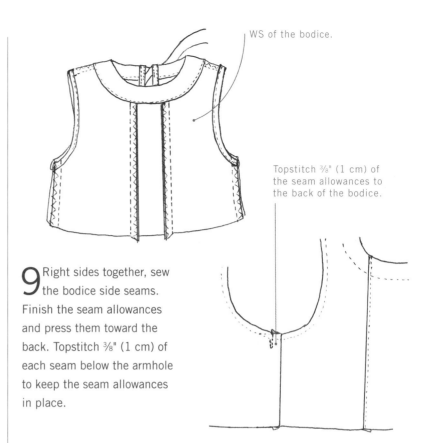

WS of the bodice.

Topstitch ⅜" (1 cm) of the seam allowances to the back of the bodice.

9 Right sides together, sew the bodice side seams. Finish the seam allowances and press them toward the back. Topstitch ⅜" (1 cm) of each seam below the armhole to keep the seam allowances in place.

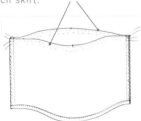

Sew two lines of gathering stitches along the top of each skirt.

10 Right sides together, sew the skirt side seams. Finish the seam allowances and press them toward the back. Press under and sew a double ⅝" (1.5 cm) hem around the bottom edge of the skirt. Gather (see page 139 for technique) the top edge of the skirt to fit the lower edge of the bodice.

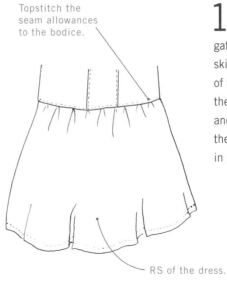

Topstitch the seam allowances to the bodice.

RS of the dress.

11 Right sides together, pin the gathered edge of the skirt to the lower edge of the bodice. Neaten the seam allowances and press them upward, then topstitch them in place.

Boy's shirt

FABRIC

Lightweight plain cotton, 57 x 23:23¾:24½:26½"
   (145 x 58:60:62:67 cm)

OTHER MATERIALS

Lightweight fusible interfacing, 2 x 8" (5 x 20 cm)
Buttons ⅜" (1 cm) diameter, 2
Sewing thread to match fabric

TECHNIQUES

Attaching facings (page 138).
Making box pleats (page 137).

PATTERN PIECES

See pattern sheet G.
All pieces cut on straight grain unless otherwise specified.
Seam allowances are ⅜" (1 cm) unless otherwise stated.
Sample is size 2 (see page 142).
The back, back yoke, and sleeve are shared with the
   Girl's Shirt (see page 70).

PATTERN PIECES IN BOOK POCKET

1 Front: cut 1 on the fold from fabric
2 Front yoke: cut 2 from fabric
3 Front yoke facing: cut 2 from fabric
4 Sleeve: cut 2 from fabric
5 Back: cut 1 on the fold from fabric
6 Back yoke: cut 1 on the fold from fabric
7 Back yoke facing: cut 1 on the fold from fabric

PATTERN PIECES TO BE MEASURED OUT

Front yoke interfacing: 1 x 7¼:7½:7¾:8"
   (2.5 x 18.5:19:19.5:20 cm), cut 2

FABRIC LAYOUT

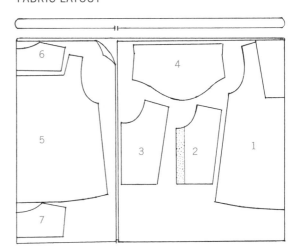

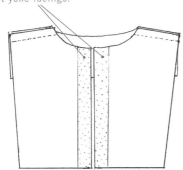

Interfacing is on the WS of the front yoke facings.

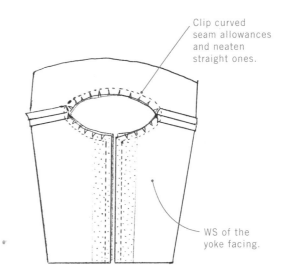

Clip curved seam allowances and neaten straight ones.

WS of the yoke facing.

1 Iron the interfacing pieces onto the wrong side of the front edges of the front yoke facings. Right sides together, sew the yoke facings together at the shoulder seams. Neaten the seam allowances and press them open. Repeat with the yokes.

2 Right sides together, pin the yoke facing to the yoke, matching all raw edges. Sew up the center front of one side, around the neck, then down the other side of the center front. Clip the curves, neaten the seam allowances, and turn the yoke facing to the inside (see page 138 for technique).

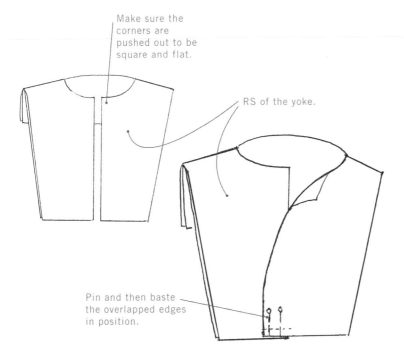

Make sure the corners are pushed out to be square and flat.

RS of the yoke.

Pin and then baste the overlapped edges in position.

3 Push the square corners out neatly and press the whole yoke section, making sure the layers are flat and aligned. Overlap the bottom edges of the front yoke (left-hand edge on top) by ⅝" (1.5 cm) and baste in position.

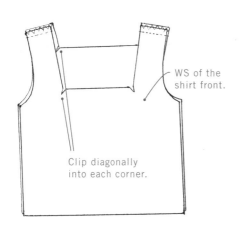

WS of the
shirt front.

Clip diagonally
into each corner.

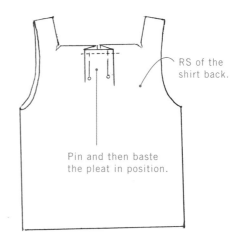

RS of the
shirt back.

Pin and then baste
the pleat in position.

4 Right sides together, sew the front and
back together at the side seams. Neaten the
seam allowances and press them toward the back.
Clip the upper corners of the front and back,
cutting in ⁵⁄₁₆" (0.8 cm).

5 Using 2⅜" (6 cm) of fabric and the marks
on the pattern piece, make a box pleat (see
page 137 for technique) in the middle of the
upper edge of the back. Baste the pleat in place
⁵⁄₁₆" (0.8 cm) from the raw edge.

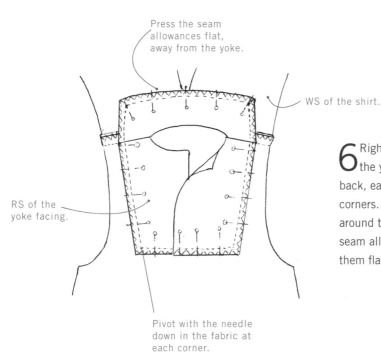

Press the seam
allowances flat,
away from the yoke.

WS of the shirt.

RS of the
yoke facing.

Pivot with the needle
down in the fabric at
each corner.

6 Right sides together, pin
the yoke to the front and
back, easing to fit at the
corners. Sew the seam all
around the yoke, neaten the
seam allowances, and press
them flat.

WS of the shirt.

Sew the hem close to the upper folded edge.

7 Right sides together, sew the front and back together at the side seams. Neaten the seam allowances and press them toward the back. Press under a ⅜" (1 cm) then a ⅝" (1.5 cm) hem around the lower edge, and then sew the hem in place.

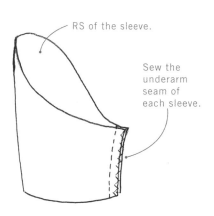

RS of the sleeve.

Sew the underarm seam of each sleeve.

8 Press under a double ⅜" (1 cm) hem on each sleeve. Unfold the hems and, right side in, sew the underarm seam. Neaten the seam allowances and press them toward the back.

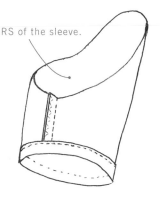

RS of the sleeve.

9 Refold the hems and sew them in place.

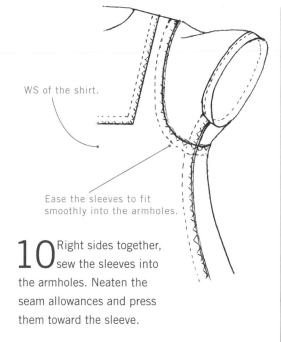

WS of the shirt.

Ease the sleeves to fit smoothly into the armholes.

10 Right sides together, sew the sleeves into the armholes. Neaten the seam allowances and press them toward the sleeve.

11 Make buttonholes in the left-hand front yoke opening as marked on the pattern. Sew on buttons to align with the buttonholes.

Girl's shirt

FABRIC
Lightweight plain cotton, 57 x 23:23¾:24:26½"
  (145 x 58:60:61:67 cm)

OTHER MATERIALS
Lightweight fusible interfacing, 2 x 6¼" (5 x 16 cm)
Button ⅜" (1 cm) diameter, 1
Sewing thread to match fabric

TECHNIQUES
Attaching facings (page 138).
Gathering (page 139).
Feather stitch (page 141).

PATTERN PIECES
See pattern sheet G.
All pieces cut on straight grain unless otherwise specified.
Seam allowances are ⅜" (1 cm) unless otherwise stated.
Sample is size 3 (see page 142).
The back, back yoke, and sleeve are shared with the
  Boy's Shirt (see page 66).

PATTERN PIECES IN BOOK POCKET
1 Front: cut 1 on the fold from fabric
2 Front yoke: cut 2 from fabric
3 Front yoke facing: cut 2 from fabric
4 Sleeve: cut 2 from fabric
5 Back: cut 1 on the fold from fabric

6 Back yoke: cut 1 on the fold from fabric
7 Back yoke facing: cut 1 on the fold from fabric

PATTERN PIECES TO BE MEASURED OUT
Front yoke interfacing: 2 x 5½:5¾:6:6⅛"
  (2.5 x 14:14.5:15:15.5 cm), cut 2

FABRIC LAYOUT

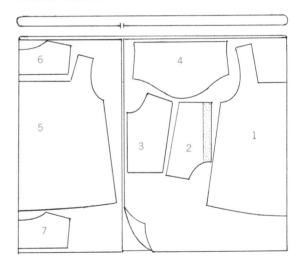

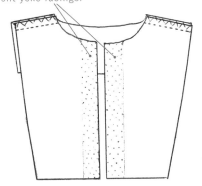

Interfacing is on the WS of the front yoke facings.

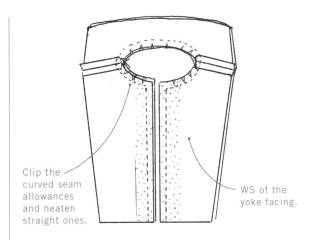

Clip the curved seam allowances and neaten straight ones.

WS of the yoke facing.

1 Iron the interfacing pieces onto the wrong side of the front edges of the front yoke facings. Right sides together, sew the yoke facings together at the shoulder seams. Neaten the seam allowances and press them open. Repeat with the yokes.

2 Right sides together, pin the yoke facing to the yoke, matching all raw edges. Sew up the center front of one side, around the neck, then down the other side of the center front. Clip the curves, neaten the seam allowances and turn the yoke facing to the inside (see page 138 for technique).

3 Push the corners out neatly and press the whole yoke section, making sure the layers are flat and aligned. Overlap the bottom edges of the front yoke (right-hand edge on top) by ⅝" (1.5 cm) and baste in position.

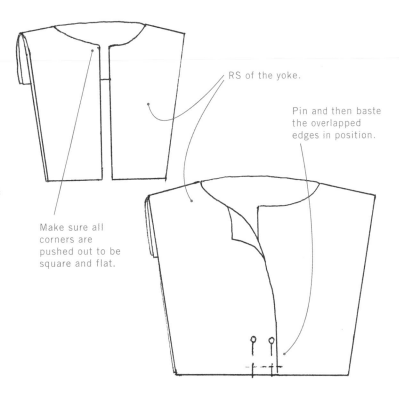

RS of the yoke.

Pin and then baste the overlapped edges in position.

Make sure all corners are pushed out to be square and flat.

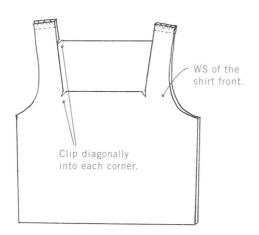

WS of the
shirt front.

Clip diagonally
into each corner.

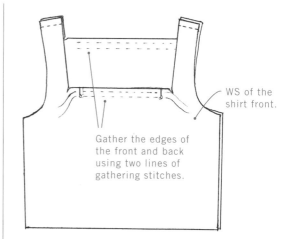

WS of the
shirt front.

Gather the edges of
the front and back
using two lines of
gathering stitches.

4 Right sides together, sew the front and
back together at the side seams. Neaten the
seam allowances and press them toward the back.
Clip the upper corners of the front and back, cutting
in ⁵⁄₁₆" (0.8 cm).

5 Gather (see page 139 for technique) the upper
edge of the back between the notches and pull
the gathers up so that the edge matches the lower
edge of the back yoke. Repeat on the upper edge of
the front to match the lower edge of the front yoke.

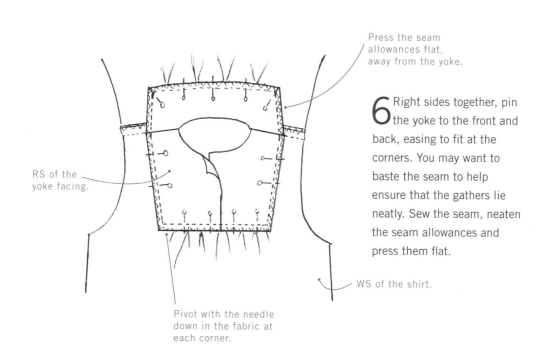

Press the seam
allowances flat,
away from the yoke.

RS of the
yoke facing.

6 Right sides together, pin
the yoke to the front and
back, easing to fit at the
corners. You may want to
baste the seam to help
ensure that the gathers lie
neatly. Sew the seam, neaten
the seam allowances and
press them flat.

WS of the shirt.

Pivot with the needle
down in the fabric at
each corner.

7 Right sides together, sew the front and back together at the side seams. Neaten the seam allowances and press them toward the back. Press under a ⅜" (1 cm) then a ⅝" (1.5 cm) hem around the lower edge, then sew the hem in place.

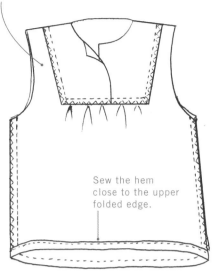

WS of the shirt.

Sew the hem close to the upper folded edge.

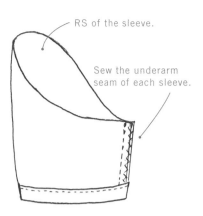

RS of the sleeve.

Sew the underarm seam of each sleeve.

8 Press under a double ⅜" (1 cm) hem on each sleeve. Unfold the hems and, right sides in, sew the underarm seams. Neaten the seam allowances and press them toward the back.

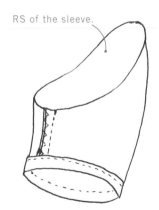

RS of the sleeve.

9 Refold the hems and sew them in place.

10 Right sides together, sew the sleeves into the armholes. Neaten the seam allowances and press them toward the sleeve.

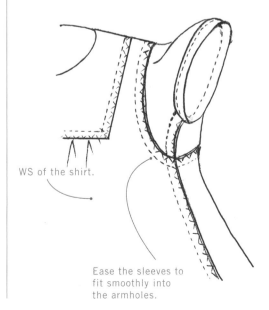

WS of the shirt.

Ease the sleeves to fit smoothly into the armholes.

11 Make a buttonhole in the right-hand front yoke opening as marked on the pattern. Sew on button to align with buttonhole. Embroider vertical bands of feather stitch (see page 141 for technique) onto the yoke if you wish.

Boy's shorts

FABRIC

Lightweight plain cotton, 61 x 24½:26:27½:29"
  (155 x 62:66:70:74 cm)

OTHER MATERIALS

Lightweight fusible interfacing, 2⅜ x ¾" (6 x 2 cm)
Cotton tape ⅝" (1.5 cm) wide, 37¾:39¾:41¼:43"
  (96:101:105:109 cm)
Sewing thread to match fabric

TECHNIQUES

Making a patch pocket (page 139).

PATTERN PIECES

See pattern sheet C.
All pieces cut on straight grain unless otherwise specified.
Seam allowances are ⅜" (1 cm) unless otherwise stated.
Sample is size 2 (see page 142).
Front and back yoke patterns are given as
  half-width, but should be traced off to produce
  full-width patterns to follow fabric layout shown.

PATTERN PIECES IN BOOK POCKET

1 Back: cut 2 from fabric
2 Front: cut 2 from fabric
3 Pocket: cut 2 from fabric
4 Front yoke: cut 1 on the bias from fabric
5 Back yoke: cut 1 on the bias from fabric

PATTERN PIECES TO BE MEASURED OUT

6 Waistband: 2 x 24½:26:27½:29" (5 x 62:66:70:74 cm),
  cut 1 from fabric
Waistband interfacing: 2⅜ x ¾" (6 x 2 cm), cut 1

FABRIC LAYOUT

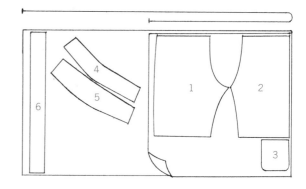

WS of the yoke.

Topstitch the seam
allowances $1/16$–$1/8$"
(2–3 mm) from the seam.

RS of the yoke.

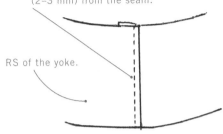

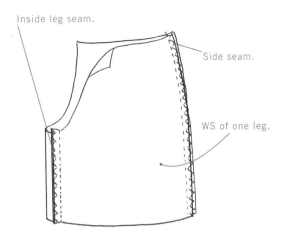

Inside leg seam.

Side seam.

WS of one leg.

1 Right sides together, sew the yokes together
at the side seams. Neaten the seam
allowances and press them toward the back,
then topstitch them in place.

2 Right sides together, sew one front and one
back together along the inside leg seam and the
side seam. Neaten all seam allowances and press
them toward the back. Repeat with the other front
and back.

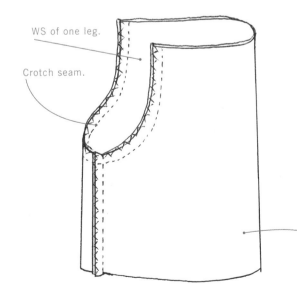

WS of one leg.

Crotch seam.

3 Turn one leg right side out
and slip it inside the other
leg, matching all seams and raw
edges. Right sides together, sew
the crotch seam and neaten the
seam allowances.

WS of other leg.

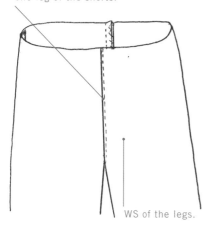

Topstitch the crotch seam allowances to one leg of the shorts.

WS of the legs.

4 Turn right side out, press the crotch seam allowances to one side and topstitch them in place.

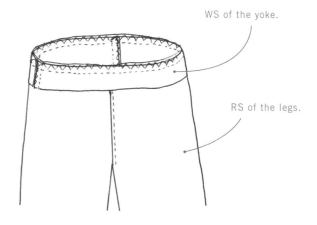

WS of the yoke.

RS of the legs.

5 Sew the lower edge of the yoke to the top edge of the shorts. Neaten the seam allowance and press the yoke and the seam allowance upward, then topstitch the seam allowance in place.

RS of the yoke.

Topstitch $1/16$–$1/8$" (2–3 mm) from the seam.

6 Make up both patch pockets (see page 139 for technique). Sew the pockets onto the back of the shorts as marked on the pattern.

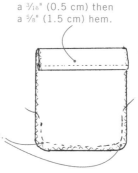

Turn under and sew a $3/16$" (0.5 cm) then a $5/8$" (1.5 cm) hem.

Turn under $1/4$" (0.7 cm) around raw edges.

Sew a line of gathering stitches around each curve.

Pull up the gathers smoothly.

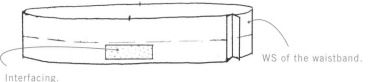

Interfacing.

WS of the waistband.

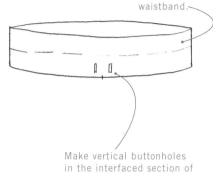

RS of the waistband.

Make vertical buttonholes in the interfaced section of the waistband.

7 Right sides together, sew the short ends of the waistband together and press the seam allowances open. Iron the strip of interfacing onto the waistband, positioning it across the center front, ⅜" (1 cm) up from the lower raw edge. Make two buttonholes in the interfaced section, each ⁹⁄₁₆" (1.3 cm) long and positioned ½" (1.2 cm) up from the raw edge of the fabric. Space the buttonholes ¾" (2 cm) apart.

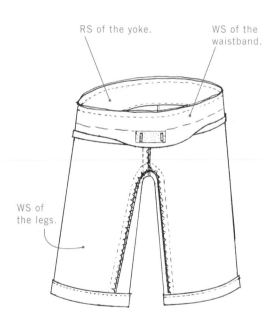

RS of the yoke.

WS of the waistband.

WS of the legs.

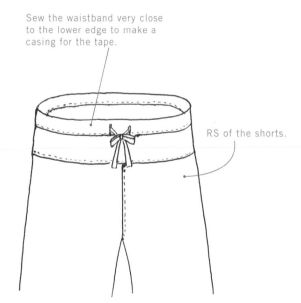

Sew the waistband very close to the lower edge to make a casing for the tape.

RS of the shorts.

8 With the right side of the waistband against the wrong side of the legs, sew the waistband to the top edge of the yoke. Press under a ⅜" (1 cm) hem around the raw edge of the waistband, then press the waistband and the seam allowance upward. Press under a ⅜" (1 cm) then a ⅝" (1.5 cm) hem around the bottom of each leg and sew it in place.

9 Fold the waistband in half to the wrong side, so the hem just overlaps the seam allowance, and topstitch it in place. Thread the cotton tape through the buttonholes and casing.

Side-button skirt

FABRIC

Lightweight plain cotton, 61 x 25¼:27½:30:32½"
(155 x 64:70:76:82 cm)

OTHER MATERIALS

Lightweight fusible interfacing, 6 x 2⅜" (15 x 6 cm)

Buttons ½" (1.2 cm) diameter, 4

Cotton tape ⅝" (1.5 cm) wide, 42:43¾:45¼:47"
(107:111:115:119 cm)

Sewing thread to match fabric

TECHNIQUES

Gathering (page 139).

PATTERN PIECES

All pieces cut on straight grain unless otherwise specified.
Seam allowances are ⅜" (1 cm) unless otherwise stated.
Sample is size 3 (see page 142).

PATTERN PIECES IN BOOK POCKET

None

PATTERN PIECES TO BE MEASURED OUT

1 Front skirt: 25¼:26:26¾:27½ x 12½:13¾:15:16¼"
(64:66:68:70 x 32:35:38:41 cm), cut 1 on the fold
from fabric

2 Back skirt: 24½:25¼:26:26¾ x 12½:13¾:15:16¼"
(62:64:66:68 x 32:35:38:41 cm), cut 1 on the fold
from fabric

3 Yoke: 11:12:12½:13½ x 2:2⅜:2¾:3⅛" (28:30:32:34 x
5:6:7:8 cm), cut 2 on the bias from fabric

4 Waistband: 21¼:23:24½:26 x 2" (54:58:62:66 x 5 cm),
cut 1 from fabric

5 Button flap: 6 x 2⅜" (15 x 6 cm), cut 1 from fabric

Placket interfacing: 4 x ¾" (10 x 2 cm), cut 1

Button flap interfacing: 6 x 2⅜" (15 x 6 cm), cut 1

Yoke interfacing: ¾ x 2:2⅜:2¾:3⅛" (2 x 5:6:7:8 cm),
cut 1

FABRIC LAYOUT

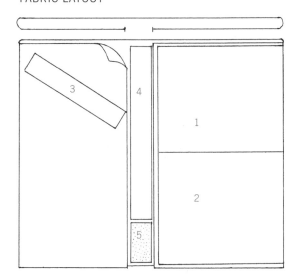

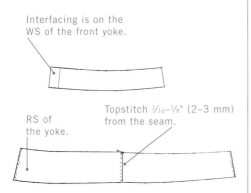

Interfacing is on the WS of the front yoke.

RS of the yoke.

Topstitch $\frac{1}{16}$–$\frac{1}{8}$" (2–3 mm) from the seam.

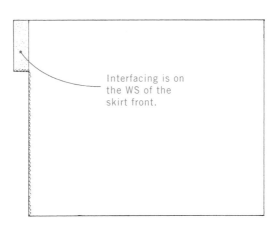

Interfacing is on the WS of the skirt front.

1 Iron the yoke interfacing onto the wrong side of the left-hand end of the front yoke. Right sides together, sew the yokes together at the right-hand side seam. Neaten the seam allowances and press them toward the back, then topstitch them in place. Neaten the short raw edge of the back yoke.

2 Starting at the lower edge, cut off a $\frac{3}{4}$" (2 cm) wide strip from the left-hand edge of the skirt front, stopping 4" (10 cm) from the top edge. You should have a 4 x $\frac{3}{4}$" (10 x 2 cm) placket strip remaining at the top of the left-hand side seam of the skirt front. (Be sure to cut this strip off the correct side of the skirt front: it should be the left-hand side as the skirt is worn.) Iron the placket interfacing onto the wrong side of the placket strip. Neaten the cut edge, as shown.

Gather the top edge between the notches marked on the pattern.

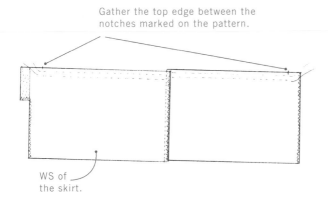

WS of the skirt.

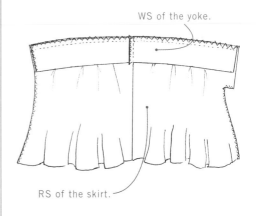

WS of the yoke.

RS of the skirt.

3 Right sides together, sew the front and back together at the right-hand side seam. Neaten the seam allowances and press them toward the back. Neaten the raw side seam allowances of both skirts. Gather (see page 139 for technique) the top edges of the skirt between the notches. Pull up the gathers to fit the lower edge of the yoke.

4 Right sides together, sew the gathered edge of the skirt to the lower edge of the yoke. Neaten the seam allowance.

Topstitch ¹⁄₁₆–¹⁄₈" (2–3 mm) from the seams.

RS of the skirt.

Sew the seam, starting ³⁄₈" (1 cm) above the lower end of the placket.

WS of the skirt.

5 Press the yoke and the seam allowance upward, then topstitch the seam allowance in place. Topstitch the seam allowance of the side seam to the skirt back.

6 Right sides together, sew the left-hand side seam from ³⁄₈" (1 cm) above the end of the placket to the lower edge of the skirt.

Topstitch the edge of the placket to the yoke and skirt.

WS of the skirt.

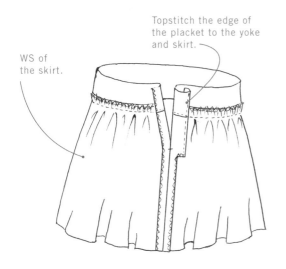

Interfacing is on the WS of the button flap.

Push out the corner so it is neat and square.

RS of the button flap.

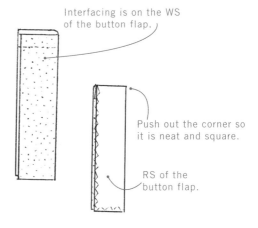

7 Press the seam allowances open, pressing the placket flat. Press under ³⁄₈" (1 cm) along the long edge of the placket and topstitch it in place to the yoke and skirt.

8 Iron the button flap interfacing onto the wrong side of the button flap. Right sides together, fold it in half vertically and sew across the top, ³⁄₈" (1 cm) from the raw edge. Turn the button flap right side out, pushing the corner out neatly, and press, making sure the layers are flat and aligned. Overlock or zig-zag stitch the raw edges together.

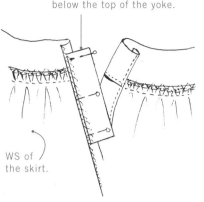

The top of the button flap should be ½" (1.2 cm) below the top of the yoke.

WS of the skirt.

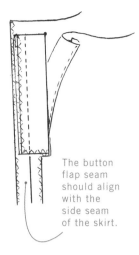

The button flap seam should align with the side seam of the skirt.

9 Pin the button flap to the seam allowance of the back skirt, at the open section of the left-hand side seam. Align the bottom of the flap with the bottom of the placket (so that the top of the flap is ½" (1.2 cm) below the top of the yoke), and match the neatened edge of the flap with the neatened edge of the seam allowance. Sew the flap in position, taking a ⅜" (1 cm) seam allowance.

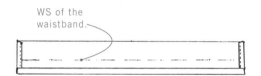

WS of the waistband.

10 Press under a double ⅜" (1 cm) hem at each short end of the waistband and sew it in place. Wrong sides together, fold the waistband in half lengthwise and press. Open it out and press under a ⅜" (1 cm) hem along one long edge.

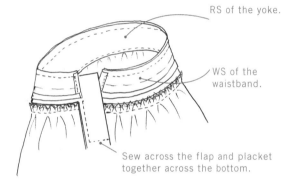

RS of the yoke.

WS of the waistband.

Sew across the flap and placket together across the bottom.

11 Pin the right side of the waistband to the wrong side of the yoke, matching the raw edges. Sew the seam. Note that the waistband does not cover the top edge of the button flap. Align the flap and placket on top of one another and sew them together across the bottom.

Sew the waistband very close to the lower edge to make a casing for the tape.

RS of the skirt.

12 Press the waistband and the seam allowance upward. Fold the waistband in half to the right side, so the hem just overlaps the seam allowance, and topstitch it in place. Thread the cotton tape through the casing. Press under a ⅜" (1 cm) then a ⅝" (1.5 cm) hem around the bottom of the skirt and sew it in place.

13 Make buttonholes in the placket as marked on the pattern. Sew buttons onto the button flap to align with the buttonholes.

Linen dress

FABRIC
Lightweight linen, 61 x 27¼:29½:32:34"
  (155 x 69:75:81:86 cm)

OTHER MATERIALS
Lightweight fusible interfacing, 12½ x 14½" (32 x 37 cm)
Buttons ½" (1.2 cm) diameter, 12
Bias binding ¾" (2 cm) wide, 25¼:26¾:28½:30"
  (64:68:72:76 cm)
Sewing thread to match fabric

TECHNIQUES
Binding an armhole (page 135).
Gathering (page 139).

PATTERN PIECES
See pattern sheet B.
All pieces cut on straight grain unless otherwise specified.
Seam allowances are ⅜" (1 cm) unless otherwise stated.
Sample is size 3 (see page 142).
The button tabs are shared with the Boy's Linen Shirt
  (see page 86).

PATTERN PIECES IN BOOK POCKET
1 Back bodice: cut 1 on the fold from fabric
2 Front bodice: cut 2 from fabric
3 Front neck facing: cut 2 from fabric + 2 interfacing

4 Back neck facing: cut 1 on the fold from fabric
  + 1 interfacing
5 Button tabs: cut 4 from fabric

PATTERN PIECES TO BE MEASURED OUT
6 Skirt: 28½:30¾:33:35½ x 12:13:14¼:15½"
  (72:78:84:90 x 30:33:36:39 cm), cut 2 on the fold
  from fabric
Placket interfacing: 2¾ x 13¾:14:14¼:14⅜"
  (7 x 35:35.5:36:36.5 cm), cut 2

FABRIC LAYOUT

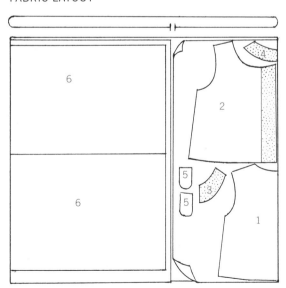

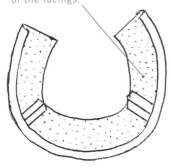

Interfacing is on the WS of the facings.

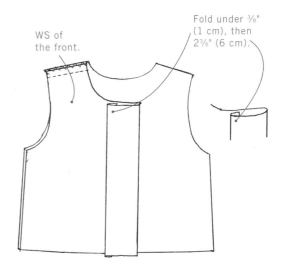

WS of the front.

Fold under ⅜" (1 cm), then 2⅜" (6 cm).

1 Iron the interfacing pieces onto the wrong side of all the neck facings. Sew the shoulder seams and press them open. Turn under and press ⅜" (1 cm) along the lower edge of the facing.

2 Right sides together, sew the bodice front and back together at the shoulder seams. Neaten the seam allowances and press them toward the back. Fold under ⅜" (1 cm) then 2⅜" (6 cm) along both center fronts and press the folds flat.

3 Open out the pressed folds. Lay a placket interfacing strip on the wrong side of the fabric, between the pressed lines, and iron it in place. Iron the other placket interfacing to the other front. Fold under the ⅜" (1 cm) hem again, then fold the 2⅜" (6 cm) hem to the right side. Pin the neck facing to the bodice neck, matching the raw edges and ensuring that the short edges of the facing overlap the edges of the placket. Sew from one center front, around the neck to the other center front. Clip the curves, neaten the seam allowances and turn the neck facing and placket to the wrong side, pushing the corners out neatly.

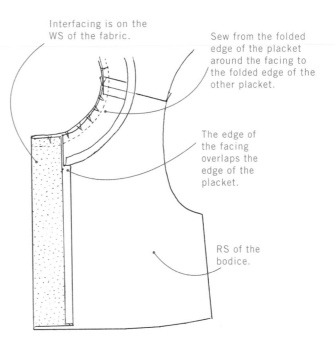

Interfacing is on the WS of the fabric.

Sew from the folded edge of the placket around the facing to the folded edge of the other placket.

The edge of the facing overlaps the edge of the placket.

RS of the bodice.

4 Press the whole section, making sure the layers are flat and aligned. Topstitch the facing and placket in place, stitching along the folded edges on the wrong side.

RS of the bodice.

It is easiest to do the topstitching from the wrong side so that you can follow the folded edges.

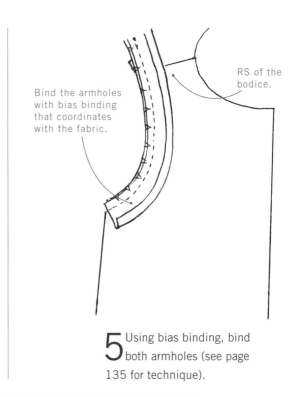

Bind the armholes with bias binding that coordinates with the fabric.

RS of the bodice.

5 Using bias binding, bind both armholes (see page 135 for technique).

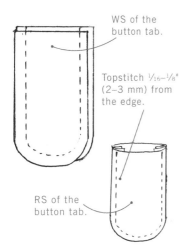

WS of the button tab.

Topstitch 1/16–1/8" (2–3 mm) from the edge.

RS of the button tab.

6 Right sides together, pair up the button tabs to make two tabs. Sew them, leaving the top straight edges open. Clip the curves, turn the tabs right side out and topstitch the seams.

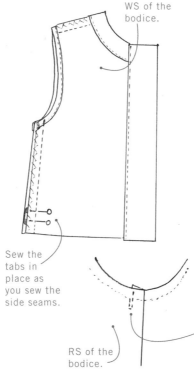

WS of the bodice.

Sew the tabs in place as you sew the side seams.

RS of the bodice.

Topstitch 3/8" (1 cm) of the seam allowances to the back of the bodice.

7 Pin the button tabs to the right side of the bodice front between the notches on the side seams. Sew the front and back bodices together at the side seams. Neaten the seam allowances and press them toward the back. Topstitch 3/8" (1 cm) of each seam below the armhole to keep the seam allowances in place, and topstitch the seam allowances over the ends of the tabs to hold them flat.

The right-hand placket (as the dress is worn) overlaps the left-hand placket.

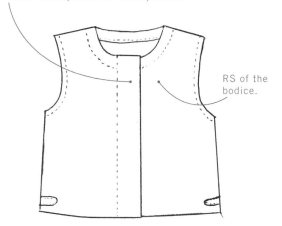

RS of the bodice.

8 Overlap the bodice center front plackets with the right-hand placket on top, and baste the bottom edge to hold them in place.

Sew two lines of gathering stitches along the top of each skirt.

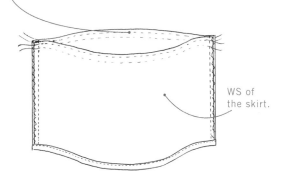

WS of the skirt.

9 Right sides together, sew the front and back skirts together at the side seams. Neaten the seam allowances and press them toward the back. Gather (see page 139 for technique) the top edge of the skirt and pull the gathers up so that the edge matches the lower edge of the bodice. Press under a ³⁄₈" (1 cm) then a ⁵⁄₈" (1.5 cm) hem around the lower edge of the skirt, then sew the hem in place.

Topstitch ¹⁄₁₆–¹⁄₈" (2–3 mm) from the seam.

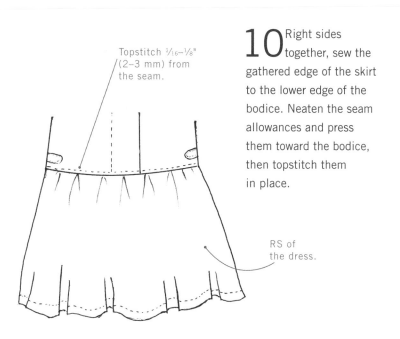

RS of the dress.

10 Right sides together, sew the gathered edge of the skirt to the lower edge of the bodice. Neaten the seam allowances and press them toward the bodice, then topstitch them in place.

11 Make buttonholes in the right-hand placket and both button tabs as marked on the pattern. Sew on buttons to align with the buttonholes. Note that the lower four buttons of the right-hand row can just be sewn on without making buttonholes if you prefer.

Boy's linen shirt

FABRIC

Lightweight linen, 61 x 19¼:20½:22:23¾"
   (155 x 49:52:56:60 cm)

OTHER MATERIALS

Lightweight fusible interfacing, 12½ x 14⅜"
   (32 x 36.5 cm)
Buttons ½" (1.2 cm) diameter, 10
Sewing thread to match fabric

PATTERN PIECES

See pattern sheets B and I.
All pieces cut on straight grain unless otherwise specified.
Seam allowances are ⅜" (1 cm) unless otherwise stated.
Sample is size 2 (see page 142).
The button tabs are shared with the Linen Dress
   (see page 82).

PATTERN PIECES IN BOOK POCKET

1 Back: cut 1 on the fold from fabric

2 Front: cut 2 from fabric

3 Sleeve: cut 2 from fabric

4 Front neck facing: cut 2 from fabric + 2 interfacing

5 Back neck facing: cut 1 on the fold from fabric
   + 1 interfacing

6 Button tabs: cut 4 from fabric

PATTERN PIECES TO BE MEASURED OUT

Placket interfacing: 2¾ x 12½:13½:14¼:15"
   (7 x 32:34:36:38 cm), cut 2

FABRIC LAYOUT

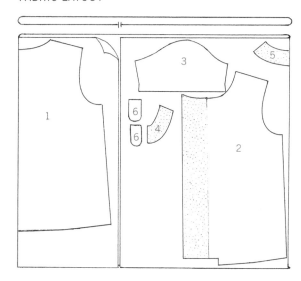

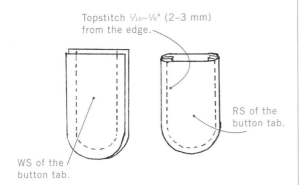

Topstitch ¹⁄₁₆–¹⁄₈" (2–3 mm) from the edge.

RS of the button tab.

WS of the button tab.

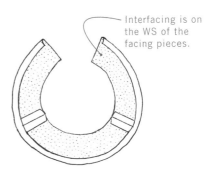

Interfacing is on the WS of the facing pieces.

1 Right sides together, pair up the button tabs to make two tabs. Sew them, leaving the top straight edges open. Clip the curves, turn the tabs right side out and topstitch the seams.

2 Iron the interfacing pieces onto the wrong side of all the neck facings. Sew the shoulder seams and press them open. Turn under and press ⅜" (1 cm) along the lower edge of the facing.

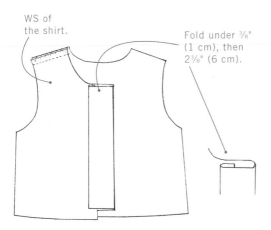

WS of the shirt.

Fold under ⅜" (1 cm), then 2⅜" (6 cm).

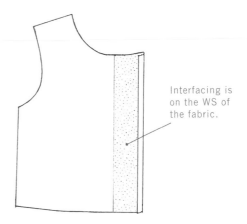

Interfacing is on the WS of the fabric.

3 Right sides together, sew the shirt front and back together at the shoulder seams. Neaten the seam allowances and press them toward the back. Fold under ⅜" (1 cm) then 2⅜" (6 cm) along both center fronts, as marked on the pattern, and press.

4 Open out the pressed folds. Lay a placket interfacing strip on the wrong side of the fabric, between the pressed lines, and iron it in place. Iron the other placket interfacing to the other front.

5 Fold under the ⅜" (1 cm) hem again, then fold the 2⅜" (6 cm) hem to the right side. Pin the neck facing to the shirt neck, matching the raw edges. Sew from one center front, around the neck to the other center front. Then sew across the bottom of the placket, ⅜" (1 cm) up from the raw edge. Clip the curves, neaten the seam allowances and turn the neck facing and placket to the wrong side, pushing the corners out neatly.

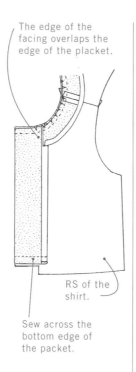

The edge of the facing overlaps the edge of the placket.

RS of the shirt.

Sew across the bottom edge of the packet.

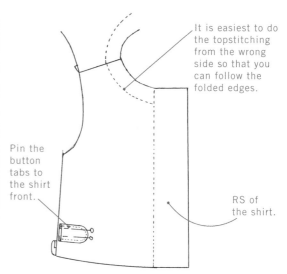

It is easiest to do the topstitching from the wrong side so that you can follow the folded edges.

Pin the button tabs to the shirt front.

RS of the shirt.

6 Press, making sure the layers are flat and aligned. Topstitch the facing and placket in place, stitching along the hems. Pin the button tabs to the right side of the shirt front between the notches on the side seams.

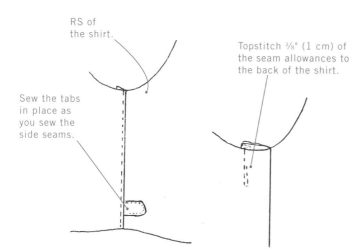

RS of the shirt.

Topstitch ⅜" (1 cm) of the seam allowances to the back of the shirt.

Sew the tabs in place as you sew the side seams.

7 Sew the front and back shirts together at the side seams. Neaten the seam allowances and press them toward the back. Topstitch close to the seams, then topstitch ⅜" (1 cm) of each seam close to the neatened edge below the armhole to keep the seam allowances in place.

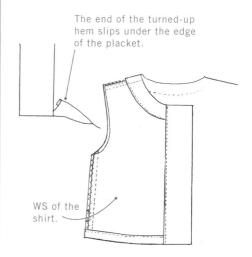

The end of the turned-up hem slips under the edge of the placket.

WS of the shirt.

8 Press under a ⅜" (1 cm) then a ⅝" (1.5 cm) hem around the lower edge of the skirt, and sew in place.

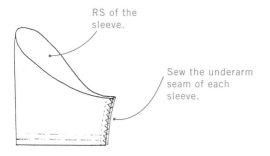

RS of the sleeve.

Sew the underarm seam of each sleeve.

9 Press under a double ⅜" (1 cm) hem on each sleeve. Unfold the hems and, right side in, sew the underarm seams. Neaten the seam allowances and press them toward the back.

10 Refold the hems and sew them in place.

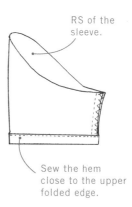

RS of the sleeve.

Sew the hem close to the upper folded edge.

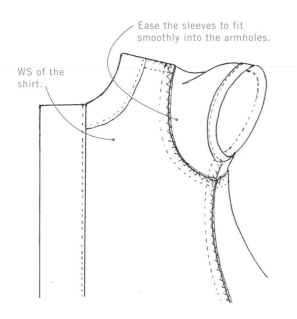

Ease the sleeves to fit smoothly into the armholes.

WS of the shirt.

11 Right sides together, sew the sleeves into the armholes. Neaten the seam allowances and press them toward the sleeve.

12 Make buttonholes in the left-hand placket and both button tabs as marked on the pattern. Sew on buttons to align with the buttonholes. Note that the lower three buttons of the right-hand row can just be sewn on without making buttonholes if you prefer.

Girl's shorts with bows

FABRIC

Lightweight plain cotton, 35 x 16½:17⅞:19¼:20¾"
  (89 x 42:45.5:49:52.5 cm)
Lightweight flowery cotton, 8¼ x 27½:29:30¾:32½"
  (21 x 70:74:78:82 cm)

OTHER MATERIALS

Lightweight fusible interfacing, 2 x 2¾" (5 x 7 cm)
Sewing thread to match fabric

TECHNIQUES

Gathering (page 139).

PATTERN PIECES

See pattern sheet A.
All pieces cut on straight grain unless otherwise specified.

Seam allowances are ⅜" (1 cm) unless otherwise stated.
Sample is size 2 (see page 142).

PATTERN PIECES IN BOOK POCKET

1 Bow: cut 2 on the fold from plain cotton
2 Bow: cut 2 on the fold from flowery cotton
3 Back: cut 2 from plain cotton
4 Front: cut 2 from plain cotton

PATTERN PIECES TO BE MEASURED OUT

5 Waistband: 27½:29:30¾:32½ x 2" (70:74:78:82 x 5 cm),
  cut 1 on the fold from plain cotton
6 Waistband facing: 27½:29:30¾:32½ x 2"
  (70:74:78:82 x 5 cm), cut 1 on the fold from flowery cotton
7 Drawstring: 1⅝ x 37¾:39½:41:42½"
  (4 x 96:100:104:108 cm), cut 1 from flowery cotton
Waistband interfacing: 2 x 2¾" (5 x 7 cm), cut 1

FABRIC LAYOUT

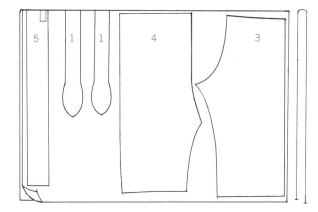
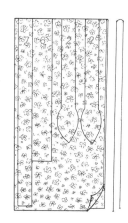

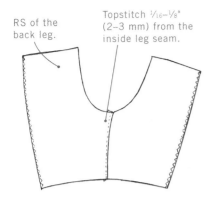

RS of the back leg.

Topstitch ¹⁄₁₆–¹⁄₈" (2–3 mm) from the inside leg seam.

1 Right sides together, sew one front and one back shorts leg together along the inside leg seams. Neaten the seam allowances and press them toward the back, then topstitch them in place. Repeat with the other front and back legs. Neaten the side seam raw edges.

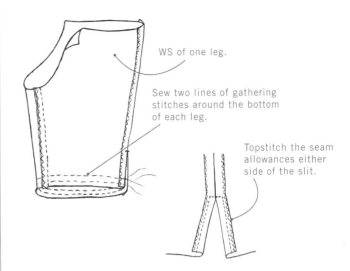

WS of one leg.

Sew two lines of gathering stitches around the bottom of each leg.

Topstitch the seam allowances either side of the slit.

2 Right sides together, sew the side seams from the top edge to the top-of-slit notch. Press the seam allowances open. Topstitch the seam allowances in place either side of the slits. Gather (see page 139 for technique) the bottom of each leg.

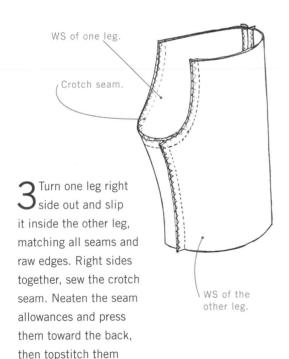

WS of one leg.

Crotch seam.

WS of the other leg.

3 Turn one leg right side out and slip it inside the other leg, matching all seams and raw edges. Right sides together, sew the crotch seam. Neaten the seam allowances and press them toward the back, then topstitch them in place.

4 Pair up a flowery and a plain bow. Right sides together, sew around the edges, leaving a gap between the notches. Clip the curves, turn right side out and press under ³⁄₈" (1 cm) across the gap. Repeat with the other flowery and plain bows.

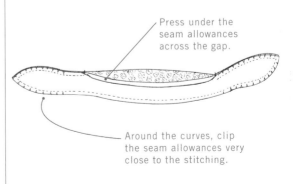

Press under the seam allowances across the gap.

Around the curves, clip the seam allowances very close to the stitching.

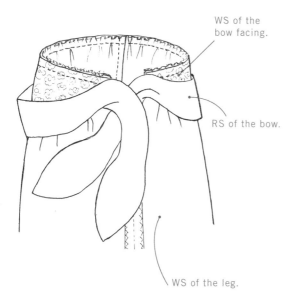

WS of the
bow facing.

RS of the bow.

WS of the leg.

5 Pull up the gathers on each leg to fit the open edge of a bow. With the facing against the wrong side of the leg, pin a bow to the bottom of each leg, matching the raw edges, and sew them in place, as shown. Press the seam allowances upward.

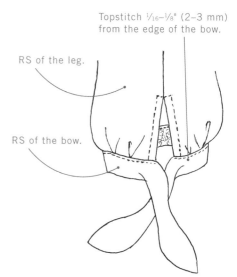

Topstitch ¹⁄₁₆–¹⁄₈" (2–3 mm) from the edge of the bow.

RS of the leg.

RS of the bow.

6 Fold the open edge of the bow over the gathered edge of the leg to the right side, and topstitch in place.

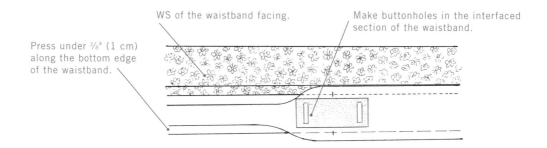

Press under ³⁄₈" (1 cm) along the bottom edge of the waistband.

WS of the waistband facing.

Make buttonholes in the interfaced section of the waistband.

7 Iron the strip of interfacing onto the waistband, positioning it across the center front, ¹¹⁄₁₆" (1.7 cm) up from the lower raw edge. Make two buttonholes in the interfaced section, each ⁵⁄₈" (1.5 cm) long and positioned ¹⁄₈" (2.5 mm) up from the bottom edge of the interfacing. Space the buttonholes 1¹⁄₈" (3 cm) apart. Sew the waistband facing to the waistband along the top long edge. Press under ³⁄₈" (1 cm) along the bottom long edge.

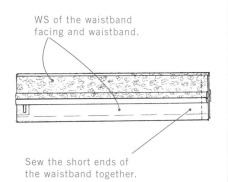

WS of the waistband facing and waistband.

Sew the short ends of the waistband together.

8 Wrong sides together, fold the waistband/facing in half along the seam and press. Open out the fold again. Right sides together, sew the short ends of the waistband/facing together and press the seam allowances open.

9 With the right side of the facing against the wrong side of the legs, sew the waistband to the top edge of the shorts, matching the waistband seam to the center back seam. Press the waistband and the seam allowance upward.

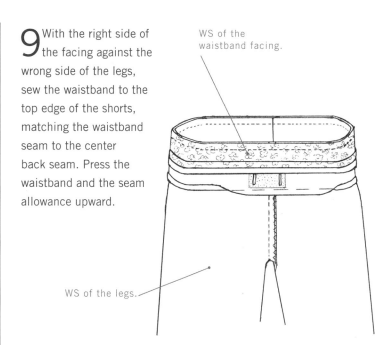

WS of the waistband facing.

WS of the legs.

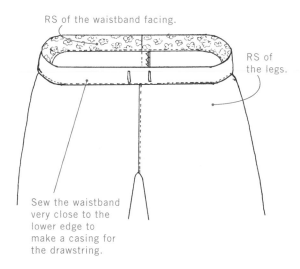

RS of the waistband facing.

RS of the legs.

Sew the waistband very close to the lower edge to make a casing for the drawstring.

10 Fold the waistband in half to the right side along the seam, so the hem just overlaps the seam allowance, and topstitch it in place.

11 Press under ⅜" (1 cm) on all edges of the drawstring. Fold it in half lengthwise and topstitch the open edges. Thread the drawstring though the buttonholes and the casing. If you prefer, you can use ⅜" (1 cm) wide cotton tape as a drawstring.

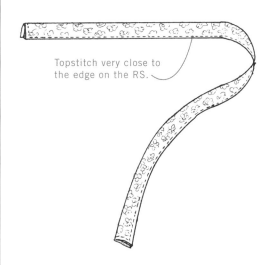

Topstitch very close to the edge on the RS.

Box-pleated dress

FABRIC

Double gauze cotton, 64½ x 40½:43¼:46½:50¾"
  (164 x 103:110:118:129 cm)

OTHER MATERIALS

Lightweight fusible interfacing, 15 x 17½:18½:19½:20½"
  (38 x 44.5:47:49.5:52 cm)

Buttons ½" (1.2 cm) diameter, 9

Sewing thread to match fabric

TECHNIQUES

Making box pleats (page 137).

Attaching facings (page 138).

PATTERN PIECES

See pattern sheet H.

All pieces cut on straight grain unless otherwise specified.

Seam allowances are ⅜" (1 cm) unless otherwise stated.

Sample is size 3 (see page 142).

Front neck facing pattern is given as half-width, but
  should be traced off to produce a full-width pattern to
  follow fabric layout shown.

The sleeve is shared with the Round-Collared Dress (see
  page 118).

PATTERN PIECES IN BOOK POCKET

1 Sleeve: cut 2 from fabric

2 Front skirt: cut 1 on the fold from fabric

3 Front bodice: cut 1 on the fold from fabric

4 Back bodice: cut 2 from fabric

5 Back skirt: cut 2 from fabric

6 Back neck facing: cut 2 from fabric + 2 interfacing

7 Front neck facing: cut 1 from fabric + 1 interfacing

PATTERN PIECES TO BE MEASURED OUT

8 Cuff: 8¼:8¾:9:9½ x 1⅝" (21:22:23:24 x 4 cm),
  cut 2 from fabric

Bodice placket interfacing: 1 x 8⅞:9½:10¼:10¾"
  (2.5 x 22.5:24:26:27.5 cm), cut 2

Skirt placket interfacing: 1 x 17¼:18¼:19¼:20¼"
  (2.5 x 44:46.5:49:51.5 cm), cut 2

FABRIC LAYOUT

Turn to page 142 for the fabric layout for this project.

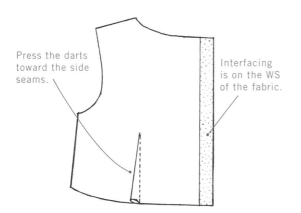

Press the darts toward the side seams.

Interfacing is on the WS of the fabric.

1 Iron the placket interfacing pieces onto the wrong side of the center back edges of both backs. Sew the back darts and press them toward the side.

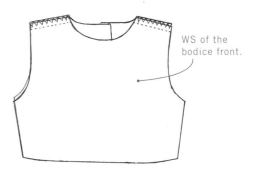

WS of the bodice front.

2 Right sides together, sew the front and back bodices together at the shoulder seams. Neaten the seam allowances and press them toward the back.

3 Press under a ⅜" (1 cm) then a ⅝" (1.5 cm) hem down both center back edges. Unfold the edges and refold them on the right side, as shown, pinning them in place.

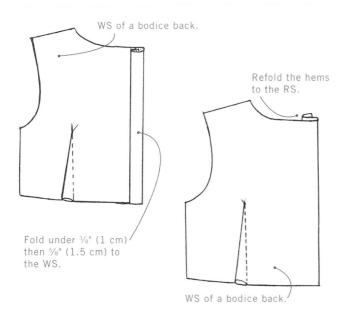

WS of a bodice back.

Refold the hems to the RS.

Fold under ⅜" (1 cm) then ⅝" (1.5 cm) to the WS.

WS of a bodice back.

Interfacing is on the WS of the facing pieces.

4 Iron the interfacing pieces onto the wrong side of all the neck facings. Sew the shoulder seams and press them open. Turn under and press ⅜" (1 cm) along the lower edge of the facing.

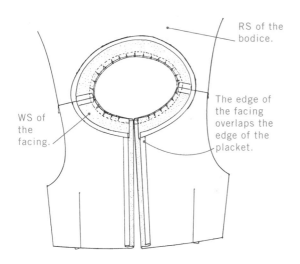

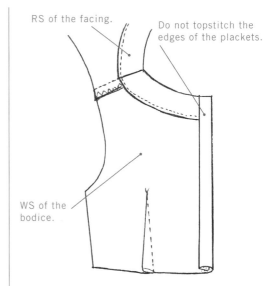

5 Right sides together, pin the neck facing to the bodice neck, matching the raw edges. Sew from one center back, around the neck to the other center back. Clip the curves, neaten the seam allowances and turn the neck facing and placket to the wrong side, pushing the corners out neatly.

6 Press, making sure the layers are flat and aligned. Topstitch the facing in place, but do not stitch along the edge of the placket.

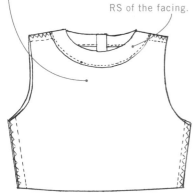

7 Right sides together, sew the front and back together at the side seams. Neaten the seam allowances and press them toward the back.

8 Fold and pin the box pleats (see page 137 for technique) on the front and back skirts as marked on the pattern. Baste the pleats in place, basting ⁵⁄₁₆" (0.8 cm) in from the edge.

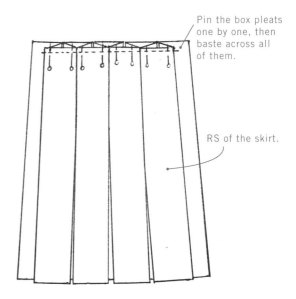

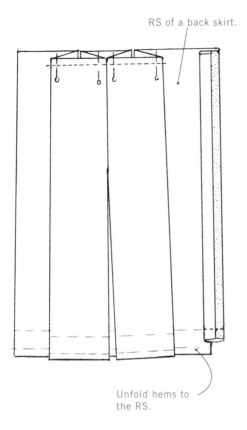

RS of a back skirt.

Unfold hems to the RS.

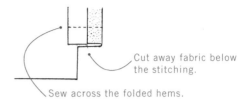

Cut away fabric below the stitching.

Sew across the folded hems.

9 Iron the placket interfacing pieces onto the wrong side of the center back edges of both back skirts. Press under a ⅜" (1 cm) then a ⅝" (1.5 cm) hem down both edges. Unfold the hems and refold them on the right side, as shown, pinning them in place. Sew across the folded hems, 1" (2.5 cm) up from the bottom edge. Cut away a square of fabric below the line of stitching, as shown, to reduce bulk. Press under a ⅜" (1 cm) then a ⅝" (1.5 cm) hem around the bottom edge of all the skirts, then unfold these hems.

10 Right sides together, sew the skirts together at the side seams. Neaten the seam allowances and press them toward the back.

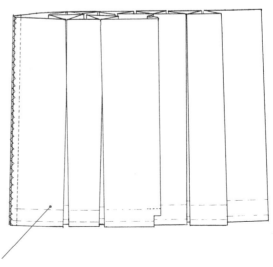

WS of a back skirt.

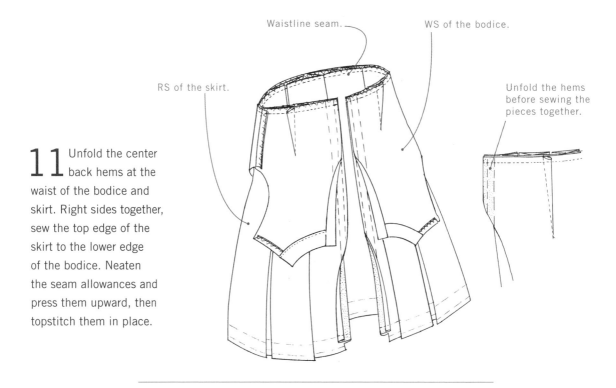

Waistline seam.

WS of the bodice.

RS of the skirt.

Unfold the hems before sewing the pieces together.

11 Unfold the center back hems at the waist of the bodice and skirt. Right sides together, sew the top edge of the skirt to the lower edge of the bodice. Neaten the seam allowances and press them upward, then topstitch them in place.

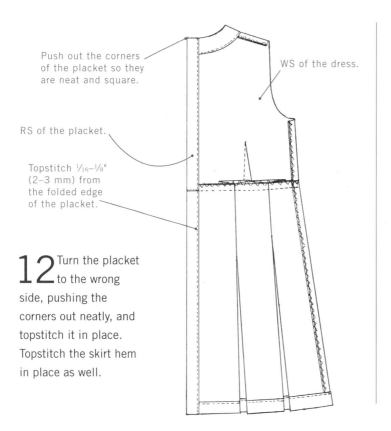

Push out the corners of the placket so they are neat and square.

WS of the dress.

RS of the placket.

Topstitch ¹⁄₁₆–¹⁄₈" (2–3 mm) from the folded edge of the placket.

12 Turn the placket to the wrong side, pushing the corners out neatly, and topstitch it in place. Topstitch the skirt hem in place as well.

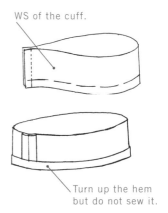

WS of the cuff.

Turn up the hem but do not sew it.

13 Press under a ³⁄₈" (1 cm) hem along one long edge of each cuff. Unfold the pressed edge and, right sides together, sew the short ends together. Press the seam allowances open and turn up the pressed hem.

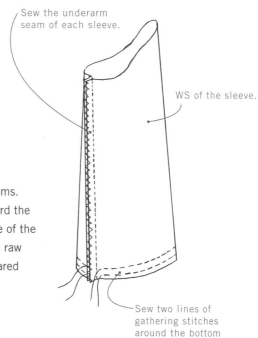

Sew the underarm seam of each sleeve.

WS of the sleeve.

Sew two lines of gathering stitches around the bottom edge of each sleeve.

14 Right sides together, sew the sleeve underarm seams. Neaten the seam allowances and press them toward the back. Gather (see page 139 for technique) the lower edge of the sleeves. Pull up the gathers so that the edge matches the raw edge of the cuffs. Follow Steps 10–12 of the Round-Collared Dress (see page 122) to attach the cuffs to the sleeves.

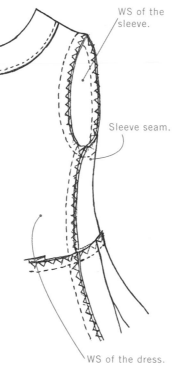

WS of the sleeve.

Sleeve seam.

WS of the dress.

15 Right sides together, slip the sleeves into the armholes, matching the raw edges. Sew the seam, then neaten the seam allowances and press them toward the sleeve.

16 Make buttonholes in the placket as marked on the pattern. Sew buttons onto the button flap to align with the buttonholes.

Shirred headband

FABRIC
Lightweight printed cotton, 8¾ x 29" (22 x 74 cm)

OTHER MATERIALS
Elastic ³⁄₁₆" (0.5 cm) wide, 83" (210 cm)
Sewing thread to match fabric
Fading fabric marker
Ruler

PATTERN PIECES
All pieces cut on straight grain unless otherwise specified. Seam allowances are ⅜" (1 cm) unless otherwise stated. Headband is one size.

PATTERN PIECES IN BOOK POCKET
None

PATTERN PIECES TO BE MEASURED OUT
Headband: 8¾ x 29" (22 x 74 cm), cut 1 from fabric

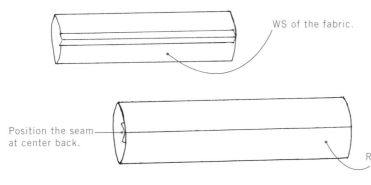

WS of the fabric.

Position the seam at center back.

RS of the fabric.

1 Right sides together, sew the long edges of the fabric together to form a tube. Press the seam allowances open and turn right side out. Roll the seam to center back and press the tube flat.

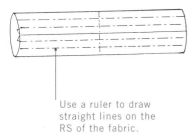

Use a ruler to draw straight lines on the RS of the fabric.

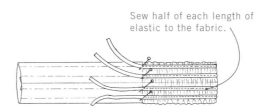

Sew half of each length of elastic to the fabric.

2 Using a fading fabric marker, mark four parallel lines on the back of the tube. Mark one line ⅜" (1 cm) in from each long edge and space the other two equally between them. Mark a vertical line down the middle of the tube.

3 Cut the elastic into four equal-length pieces. Pin the mid-point of one piece to the middle of the first horizontal line. Set the sewing machine stitch length to 4 mm (6 stitches per inch). Put the fabric under the machine and lower the needle to pierce the elastic and fabric where it's pinned. Stretch out the elastic until the cut end touches the raw end of the tube, keeping the elastic on the marked line. Pin the end in place. Keeping the tension on the elastic so that it lies flat against the fabric, sew along the center of the elastic. Repeat to sew half of each length of elastic in place.

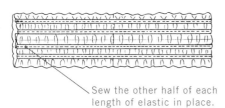

Sew the other half of each length of elastic in place.

4 Now sew the other half of each length of elastic to the fabric, from the mid-point to the other end of the fabric tube.

5 Right sides together, sew the short ends of the fabric together. Neaten the seam allowances and press them to one side, then topstitch them in place.

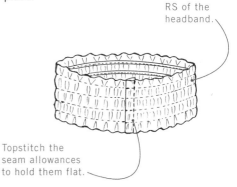

RS of the headband.

Topstitch the seam allowances to hold them flat.

Layered headband

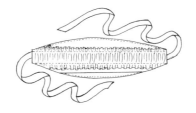

FABRIC

Double gauze cotton (pale color), 8¾ x 12" (22 x 30 cm)

Double gauze cotton (dark color), 1⅝ x 18" (4 x 46 cm)

Lightweight printed cotton, 2⅜ x 12" (6 x 30 cm)

OTHER MATERIALS

Ribbon ⅝" (1.5 cm) wide, 51" (130 cm)

Sewing thread to match fabric

Embroidery thread to match fabric

TECHNIQUES

Gathering (page 139).

Ladder stitch (page 140).

PATTERN PIECES

See pattern sheet C.

All pieces cut on straight grain unless otherwise specified.

Seam allowances are ⅜" (1 cm) unless otherwise stated.

Headband is one size.

PATTERN PIECES IN BOOK POCKET

Base: cut 2 from pale-colored double gauze

Layer 3: cut 1 from printed cotton

PATTERN PIECES TO BE MEASURED OUT

Layer 2: 18 x 1⅝" (46 x 4 cm), cut 1 from dark-colored
double gauze

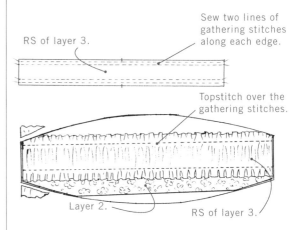

1 Right side up, pin layer 2 to the right side of one base piece, positioning it as shown. Baste the upper edge in place.

2 Gather (see page 139 for technique) the long edges of layer 3. Pull up the gathers to fit across the middle of the base piece. Right side up, pin the layer to the base and topstitch over the gathering lines to hold the layers together. Trim any protruding edges of the layered pieces to fit the base piece.

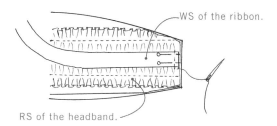

WS of the ribbon.

RS of the headband.

3 Cut the ribbon into two equal lengths. Right side down, pin one end of each length to one end of the right side of the headband, matching the raw edges as shown. Baste the ribbons in place, sewing ³⁄₁₆" (0.5 cm) in from the edge.

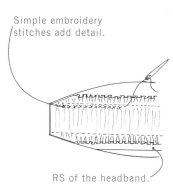

Simple embroidery stitches add detail.

RS of the headband.

4 Add simple embroidery stitches along the edge of the top layer: here, cross stitches are used.

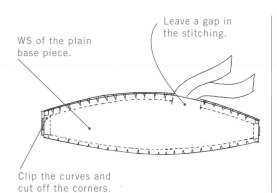

WS of the plain base piece.

Leave a gap in the stitching.

Clip the curves and cut off the corners.

5 Right sides together, lay the plain base piece over the embellished one, matching the raw edges. Sew around the edges, leaving a 2" (5 cm) gap and making sure the ribbons don't get caught in the stitching. Clip the curves and cut off the corners.

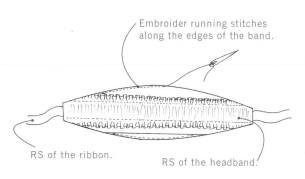

Embroider running stitches along the edges of the band.

RS of the ribbon.

RS of the headband.

6 Neaten the seam allowances and turn the headband right side out through the gap. Ladder stitch the gap closed (see page 140 for technique). Embroider both curved edges to decorate the band and to hold the layers flat.

Unisex jacket

FABRIC

Cotton jersey, 61 x 35½:38¼:41:44"
  (155 x 90:97:104:112 cm)

OTHER MATERIALS

Fusible interfacing, 15¾ x 19⅛:19¼:19½:20½"
  (40 x 48.5:49:49.5:52 cm)
Sewing thread to match fabric
1" (2.5 cm) diameter buttons, 3
¾" (2 cm) diameter button, 1

TECHNIQUES

Slip stitch (page 141).
Making a patch pocket (page 139).

PATTERN PIECES

See pattern sheets C and D.
All pieces cut on straight grain unless otherwise specified.
Seam allowances are ⅝" (1.5 cm) unless otherwise
  stated.
Sample is size 3 (see page 142).
The pocket is shared with the Boy's Raglan Jacket
  (see page 130).

PATTERN PIECES IN BOOK POCKET

1 Back: cut 1 on the fold from fabric
2 Pocket: cut 2 from fabric
3 Front: cut 2 from fabric

4 Sleeve: cut 2 from fabric
5 Collar: cut 2 on the fold from fabric + 2 interfacing

PATTERN PIECES TO BE MEASURED OUT

Placket interfacing: 2¾ x 16⅜:17¾:19⅛:20½"
  (7 x 41.5:45:48.5:52 cm), cut 2

FABRIC LAYOUT

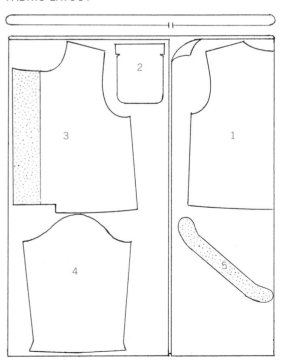

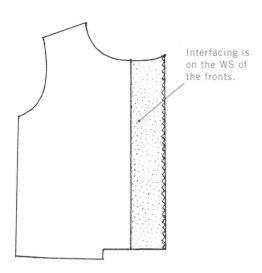

Interfacing is on the WS of the fronts.

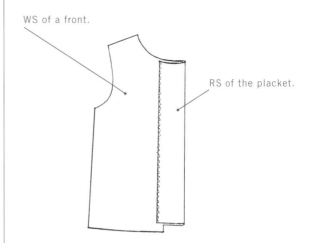

WS of a front.

RS of the placket.

1 Iron the placket interfacing pieces onto the wrong side of the center front edges of both fronts. Neaten the center front edge and the hem of the fronts and back.

2 Fold the plackets to the wrong side and press the folds.

3 Right sides together, sew the fronts and back together at the shoulder and side seams. Neaten the seam allowances and press them toward the back, then topstitch them all in place.

RS of the back.

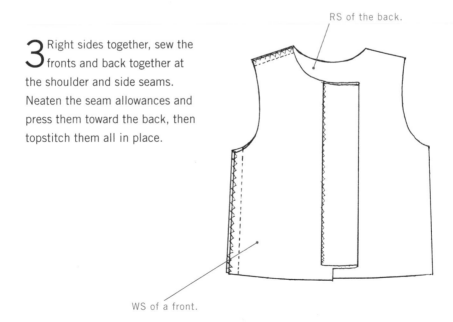

WS of a front.

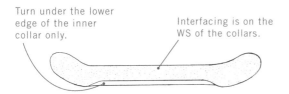

Turn under the lower edge of the inner collar only.

Interfacing is on the WS of the collars.

4 Iron interfacing onto both collars. On one piece, fold up the lower edge between the notches by ⅜" (1 cm) and press: this will be the inner collar.

5 Right sides together, sew the collars together taking a ⅜" (1 cm) seam allowance and leaving the lower edge between the notches open. Clip the curves and turn the collar right side out.

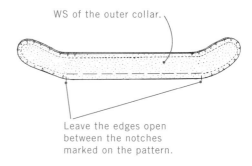

WS of the outer collar.

Leave the edges open between the notches marked on the pattern.

6 Right sides together, pin the outer collar to the fronts and back, from center front to center front. Sew the seam taking a ⅜" (1 cm) seam allowance. Clip the curves, and press the seam allowances toward the collar.

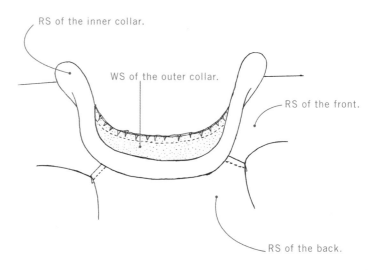

RS of the inner collar.

WS of the outer collar.

RS of the front.

RS of the back.

7 Turn the inner collar down over the seam allowances and slip stitch (see page 141 for technique) it in place along the open edge. Topstitch all around the collar.

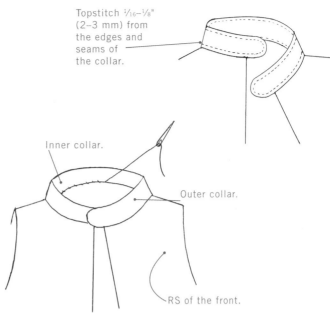

Topstitch ¹⁄₁₆–¹⁄₈" (2–3 mm) from the edges and seams of the collar.

Inner collar.

Outer collar.

RS of the front.

8 Neaten the cuff edge of both sleeves. Press under a 1" (2.5 cm) hem along both cuff edges, then unfold the hems and sew the underarm seams.

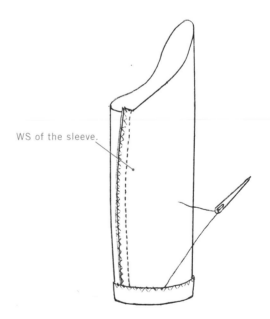

WS of the sleeve.

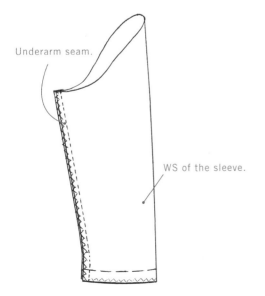

Underarm seam.

WS of the sleeve.

9 Neaten the seam allowances and press them toward the back. Refold the hems and slip stitch them in place.

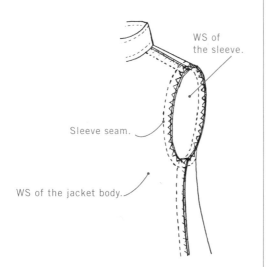

WS of
the sleeve.

Sleeve seam.

WS of the jacket body.

10 Right sides together, slip the sleeves into the armholes. Sew the seams, neaten the seam allowances and press them toward the sleeve.

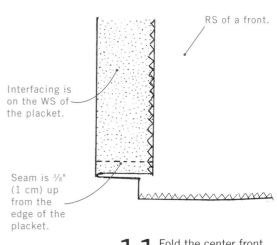

RS of a front.

Interfacing is
on the WS of
the placket.

Seam is ⅜"
(1 cm) up
from the
edge of the
placket.

11 Fold the center front plackets to the right side and sew across them, ⅜" (1 cm) up from the lower edge, as shown.

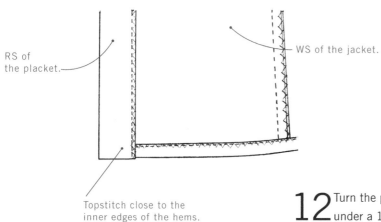

RS of
the placket.

WS of the jacket.

Topstitch close to the
inner edges of the hems.

12 Turn the plackets to the wrong side. Press under a 1" (2.5 cm) hem all around the bottom edge of the jacket. Topstitch down from the neck edge of one center front, around the hem and up to the neck edge of the other center front.

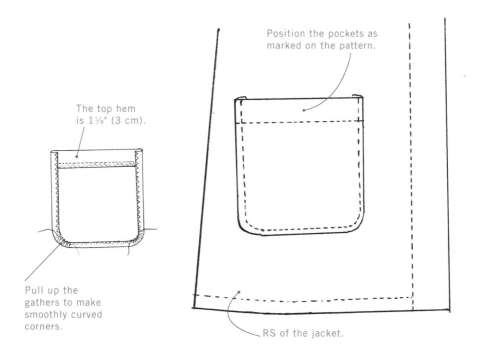

The top hem is 1⅛" (3 cm).

Pull up the gathers to make smoothly curved corners.

Position the pockets as marked on the pattern.

RS of the jacket.

13 Make up both patch pockets (see page 139 for technique). Press under a 1⅛" (3 cm) hem across the top of each pocket and sew it in place. Sew the pockets onto the front of the jacket as marked on the pattern.

14 Make buttonholes in one placket and both ends of the collar as marked on the pattern. Sew the larger buttons onto the other placket to align with the buttonholes, and to fasten the outside end of the collar. Sew on the smaller button inside the jacket to hold the inside end of the collar in place.

Jersey dress

FABRIC

Jersey fabric, 61 x 25¼:27½:29½:32"
   (155 x 64:70:75:81 cm)

OTHER MATERIALS

Lightweight fusible interfacing, 10¼ x 8¼" (26 x 21 cm)

Cotton tape 2" (5 cm) wide, 39½" (100 cm)

Bias binding ¾" (2 cm) wide, 30¼:32:33½:35"
   (77:81:85:89 cm)

Sewing thread to match fabric

TECHNIQUES

Attaching facings (page 138).

Binding an armhole (page 135).

Binding a center back opening (page 136).

Gathering (page 139).

PATTERN PIECES

See pattern sheets A and E.

All pieces cut on straight grain unless otherwise specified.

Seam allowances are ⅜" (1 cm) unless otherwise stated.

Sample is size 3 (see page 142).

The back bodice and front and back neck facings are
   shared with the Striped Dress (see page 62).

PATTERN PIECES IN BOOK POCKET

1 Back bodice: cut 1 on the fold from fabric

2 Front neck facing: cut 1 from fabric + 1 interfacing

3 Back neck facing: cut 2 from fabric + 2 interfacing

4 Front bodice: cut 1 on the fold from fabric

PATTERN PIECES TO BE MEASURED OUT

5 Skirt: 25½:26¾:28:29 x 13⅝:14¾:16:17⅛"
   (65:68:71:74 x 34.5:37.5:40.5:43.5 cm),
   cut 2 on the fold from fabric

FABRIC LAYOUT

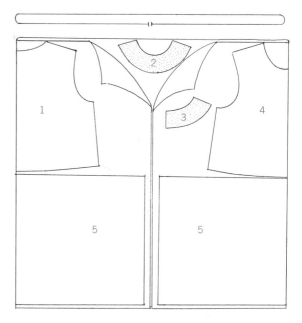

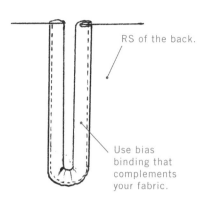

RS of the back.

Use bias binding that complements your fabric.

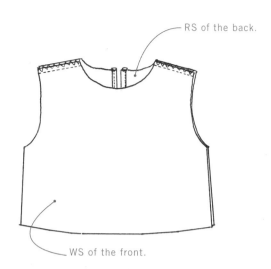

RS of the back.

WS of the front.

1 Cut open the top of the center back bodice as marked on the pattern. Using bias binding, bind the center back opening (see page 136 for technique).

2 Right sides together, sew the front and back bodices together at the shoulder seams. Neaten the seam allowances and press them toward the back.

3 Using bias binding, bind the armholes (see page 135 for technique).

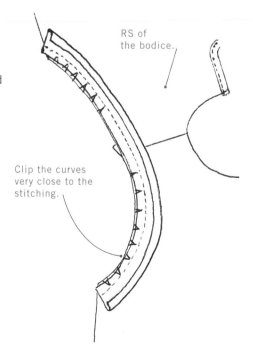

RS of the bodice.

Clip the curves very close to the stitching.

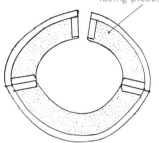

Interfacing is on
the WS of the
facing pieces.

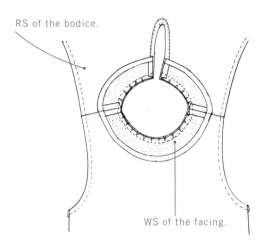

RS of the bodice.

WS of the facing.

4 Iron the interfacing pieces onto the wrong side of all the neck facings. Sew the shoulder seams and press them open. Turn under and press ⅜" (1 cm) along the lower edge of the facing and at each short end.

5 Right sides together, sew the neck facing to the bodice neck, matching the raw edges (see page 138 for technique). Clip the curves and turn the facing to the wrong side.

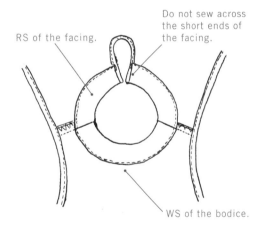

RS of the facing.

Do not sew across
the short ends of
the facing.

WS of the bodice.

6 Press, making sure the layers are aligned. Topstitch the facing in place, stitching along the edge, but do not stitch down the short ends.

7 Cut the cotton tape in half to make two ties. Pleat one end of each tie as shown (see page 137 for technique) and stitch across, ⁵⁄₁₆" (0.8 cm) from the end. Turn under and sew a double ³⁄₁₆" (0.5 cm) hem at the other end of each tie.

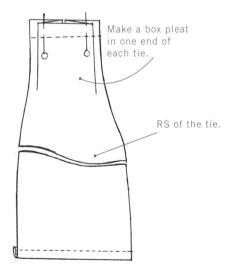

Make a box pleat
in one end of
each tie.

RS of the tie.

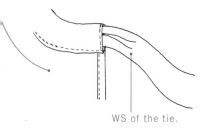

WS of the tie.

8 Tuck the pleated end of a tie under each short end of the neck facing, as shown. Topstitch down the edge of the facing, sewing the tie in place.

9 Right sides together, sew the front and back bodices together at the side seams. Neaten the seam allowances and press them toward the back. Topstitch ⅜" (1 cm) of each seam below the armhole to keep the seam allowances in place.

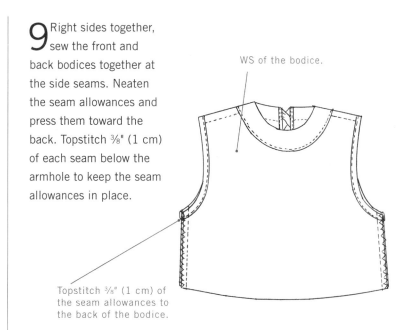

WS of the bodice.

Topstitch ⅜" (1 cm) of the seam allowances to the back of the bodice.

WS of the skirt. Sew two lines of gathering stitches along the top of each skirt.

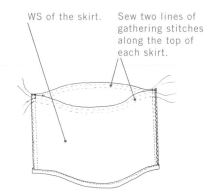

10 Right sides together, sew the skirts together at the side seams. Neaten the seam allowances and press them toward the back. Press under a ⅜" (1 cm) then a ⅝" (1.5 cm) hem around the lower edge of the skirt, then topstitch in place. Gather (see page 139 for technique) the top edge of the skirt.

11 Pull the gathers up so that the top edge of the skirt matches the lower edge of the bodice. Right sides together, pin the gathered edge of the skirt to the lower edge of the bodice. Sew the seam, neaten the seam allowances and press them toward the bodice.

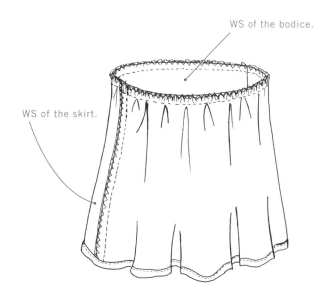

WS of the bodice.

WS of the skirt.

Skirt with bow

FABRIC

Colored double gauze cotton, 55:56¾:58¼:59¾ x
    13:14½:16¼:17¾" (140:144:148:152 x
    33:37:41:45 cm)

Lightweight cotton (for lining), 29¼:30⅛:31:31¾ x
    13½:15:16½:18" (74.5:76.5:78.5:80.5 x
    34:38:42:46 cm)

White double gauze cotton, 6 x 13:14½:16¼:17¾"
    (15 x 33:37:41:45 cm)

OTHER MATERIALS

Cotton tape 2" (5 cm) wide, 36¼" (92 cm)

Elastic ⁵⁄₁₆" (0.8 cm) wide, 37¾:39½:41:42½"
  (96:100:104:108 cm)

Sewing thread to match fabric

PATTERN PIECES

All pieces cut on straight grain unless otherwise specified.
Seam allowances are ⅜" (1 cm) unless otherwise stated.
Sample is size 3 (see page 142).

PATTERN PIECES IN BOOK POCKET
None

PATTERN PIECES TO BE MEASURED OUT
1 Skirt: 55:56¾:58¼:59¾ x 13:14½:16¼:17¾"
  (140:144:148:152 x 33:37:41:45 cm), cut 1 on
  the fold from colored double gauze
2 Lining: 29¼:30⅛:31:31¾ x 13½:15:16½:18"
  (74.5:76.5:78.5:80.5 x 34:38:42:46 cm), cut 2 from
  lightweight cotton
3 Inset: 6 x 13:14½:16¼:17¾" (15 x 33:37:41:45 cm),
  cut 1 from white double gauze

FABRIC LAYOUT

1 Cut the cotton tape in half to make two ties. Pleat one end of each tie as shown (see page 137 for technique) and stitch across, ⁵⁄₁₆" (0.8 cm) from the end. Turn under and sew a double ³⁄₁₆" (0.5 cm) hem on the other end of each tie.

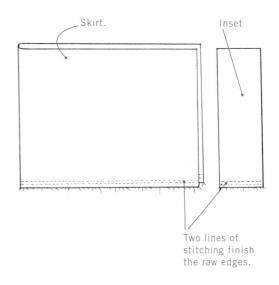

Skirt.

Inset

Two lines of stitching finish the raw edges.

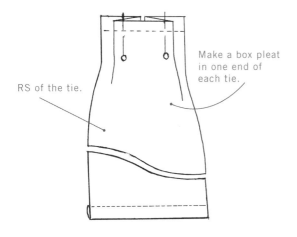

RS of the tie.

Make a box pleat in one end of each tie.

2 Sew two lines of stitches along the bottom edge of the skirt and inset. Sew the first line ³⁄₁₆" (0.5 cm) up from the raw edge and the second line ⅛" (3 mm) above the first.

3 Right sides together, sew the skirt and inset together to form a circle, as shown. Neaten the seam allowances and press them toward the skirt.

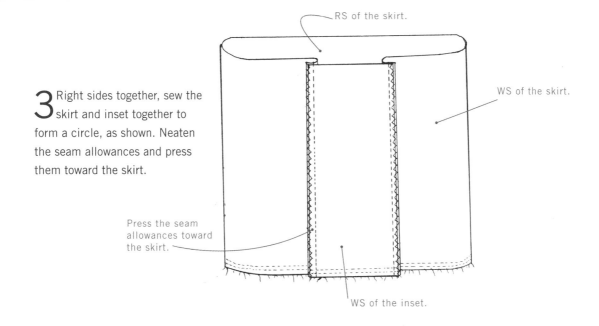

RS of the skirt.

WS of the skirt.

Press the seam allowances toward the skirt.

WS of the inset.

4 Place the pleated end of one tie square against one inset/skirt seam, 2" (5 cm) down from the top edge of the skirt. Sewing ⅝" (1.5 cm) from the seam line, sew down 3⅛" (8 cm) from the top edge, catching the tie in the stitching, as shown. Press the stitched section toward the skirt. Repeat to attach the other tie to the other side of the inset. Turn the skirt right side out.

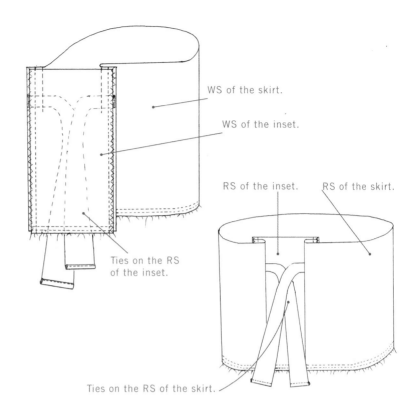

WS of the skirt.

WS of the inset.

RS of the inset.

RS of the skirt.

Ties on the RS of the inset.

Ties on the RS of the skirt.

RS of the lining.

Leave a 1" (2.5 cm) gap in the left-hand side seam.

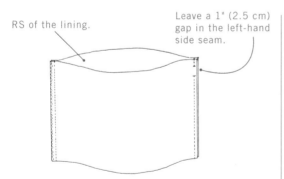

Topstitch the seam allowances to hold them flat.

WS of the lining.

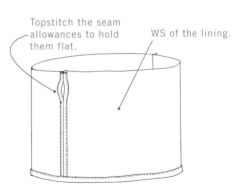

5 Sew the linings right sides together, along the right-hand side seam. Neaten the seam allowances and press them toward the back. On the left-hand side seam (the left-hand side as the skirt is worn), sew down for ⅝" (1.5 cm) from the top edge, then leave a 1" (2.5 cm) gap, then sew the rest of the seam. Press the seam allowances open.

6 Press under the raw edge of each left-hand seam allowance and topstitch them. Press under a double ⅜" (1 cm) hem around the bottom edge of the lining and sew it in place.

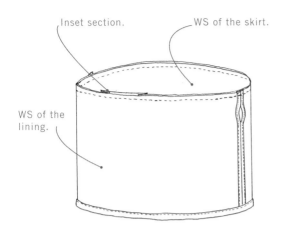

Inset section.   WS of the skirt.

WS of the lining.

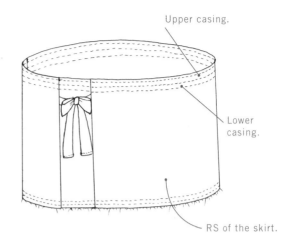

Upper casing.

Lower casing.

RS of the skirt.

7 Slip the skirt inside the lining with the right side of the lining against the right side of the skirt, matching the raw top edges. Position the inset in the skirt between the side seams of the lining. Sew the layers together around the top edge. Press the seam flat, then turn the lining to the inside.

8 Topstitch around the top of the skirt, ³⁄₁₆" (0.5 cm) down from the top edge. Sew a second then a third line of stitches, each ½" (1.2 cm) below the previous line to make two casings around the top of the skirt. Tie the tapes in a bow.

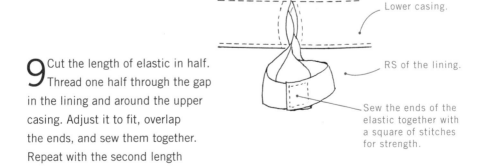

Upper casing.

Lower casing.

RS of the lining.

Sew the ends of the elastic together with a square of stitches for strength.

9 Cut the length of elastic in half. Thread one half through the gap in the lining and around the upper casing. Adjust it to fit, overlap the ends, and sew them together. Repeat with the second length in the lower casing.

Round-collared dress

FABRIC

Double gauze cotton, 61 x 37¾:41:44½:48"
  (155 x 96:104:113:122 cm)

OTHER MATERIALS

Lightweight fusible interfacing, 7 x 14:15:16¼:17⅛"
  (18 x 35.5:38:41:43.5 cm)
Bias binding 1" (2.5 cm) wide, 15½:16:16⅜:17"
  (39:40.5:41.5:43 cm)
Buttons ½" (1.2 cm) diameter, 5
Sewing thread to match fabric

TECHNIQUES

Gathering (page 139).

PATTERN PIECES

See pattern sheets B and H.
All pieces cut on straight grain unless otherwise specified.
Seam allowances are ⅜" (1 cm) unless otherwise stated.
Sample is size 3 (see page 142).
The sleeve is shared with the Box-Pleated Dress
  (see page 94).

PATTERN PIECES IN BOOK POCKET

1 Front: cut 1 on the fold from fabric
2 Back: cut 2 from fabric
3 Sleeve: cut 2 from fabric
4 Collar: cut 4 from fabric + 2 interfacing

PATTERN PIECES TO BE MEASURED OUT

5 Cuff: 8¼:8¾:9:9½ x 1⅝" (21:22:23:24 x 4 cm),
  cut 2 from fabric
6 Skirt: 32½:33½:34¾:35¾ x 11¼:12⅜:13⅝:14¾"
  (82:85:88:91 x 28.5:31.5:34.5:37.5 cm), cut 2 on
  the fold from fabric
Placket interfacing: 1 x 14:15:16:17⅛"
  (2.5 x 35.5:38:40.5:43.5 cm), cut 2

FABRIC LAYOUT

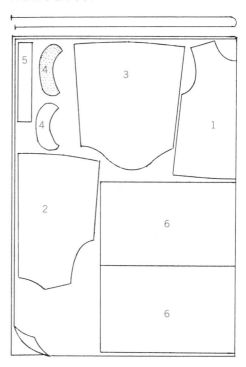

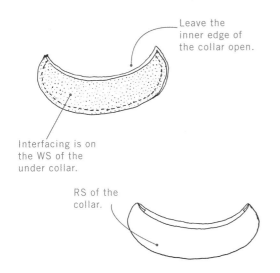

Leave the inner edge of the collar open.

Interfacing is on the WS of the under collar.

RS of the collar.

1 Iron the collar interfacing onto the wrong side of two fabric collars: these will be the under collars. Right sides together, pair a collar and under collar together and sew around the outer edge. Neaten the seam allowances, clip the curves, turn the collar right side out, and press it flat. Repeat with the other collar and under collar.

2 Right sides together, sew the front and back bodices together at the shoulder and side seams. Neaten the seam allowances and press them toward the back.

RS of the back.

WS of the front.

3 Iron the placket interfacing pieces onto the wrong side of the center back edges of both backs. Press under a ⅜" (1 cm) then a ⅝" (1.5 cm) hem down both center back edges.

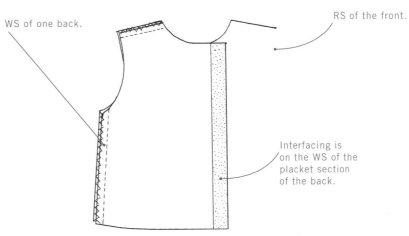

WS of one back.

RS of the front.

Interfacing is on the WS of the placket section of the back.

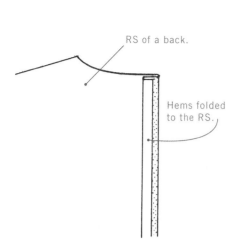

RS of a back.

Hems folded
to the RS.

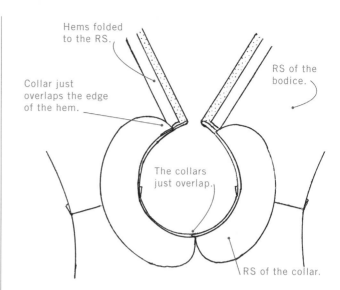

Hems folded
to the RS.

Collar just
overlaps the edge
of the hem.

RS of the
bodice.

The collars
just overlap.

RS of the collar.

4 Unfold the hems and refold them on the right side, as shown, pinning them in place.

5 Right side up, lay the collars on the right side of the bodice neck. At the center back the tips of the collars should just touch the folded-over hems, and at the front they should just overlap. Baste the collars in place, basting ⁵⁄₁₆" (0.8 cm) in from the edge.

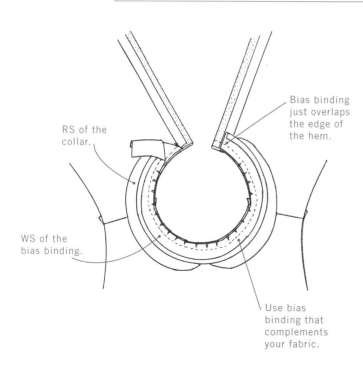

RS of the
collar.

Bias binding
just overlaps
the edge of
the hem.

WS of the
bias binding.

Use bias
binding that
complements
your fabric.

6 Lay the binding over the collars, matching the raw edges and easing it—and clipping the edge if necessary—to fit the curve. Ensure that the ends just overlap the folded edges at the center back, as shown. Sew through all layers to sew the collars and binding in place.

7 Trim the neck seam allowances down to ³⁄₁₆" (0.5 cm) on all layers. Fold the binding to the wrong side. Flip the collars toward the neck to get them out of the way, then topstitch the binding in place, making sure the collars don't get caught in the stitching. Turn the folded center back hems to the wrong side, pushing the corners out neatly, and topstitch them in place.

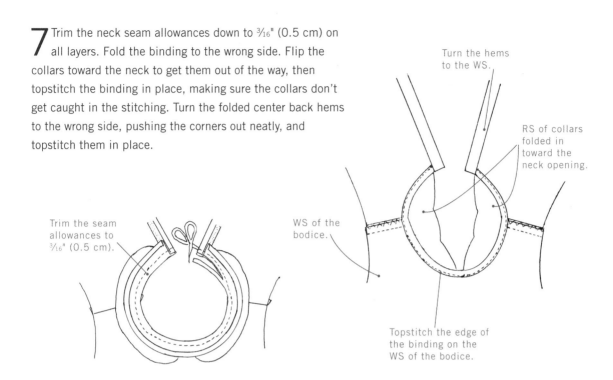

Turn the hems to the WS.

RS of collars folded in toward the neck opening.

Trim the seam allowances to ³⁄₁₆" (0.5 cm).

WS of the bodice.

Topstitch the edge of the binding on the WS of the bodice.

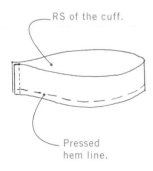

RS of the cuff.

Pressed hem line.

8 Press under a ³⁄₈" (1 cm) hem along one long edge of each cuff. Unfold the pressed edge and, right sides together, sew the short ends together. Press the seam allowances open, and then re-press the hem.

9 Right sides together, sew the sleeve underarm seams. Neaten the seam allowances and press them toward the back. Gather (see page 139 for technique) the lower edge of the sleeves. Pull up the gathers on the lower edges of the sleeves so that the edge matches the raw edge of the cuffs.

Sew two lines of gathering stitches along the bottom edge of each sleeve.

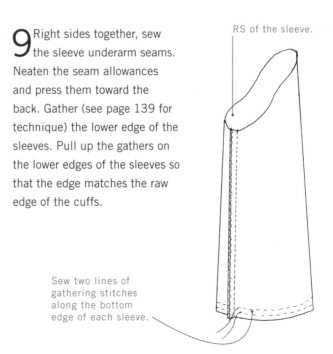

RS of the sleeve.

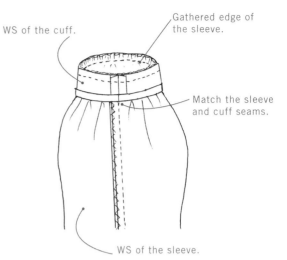

Gathered edge of the sleeve.

WS of the cuff.

Match the sleeve and cuff seams.

10 Wrong sides together, slip a cuff over the gathered edge of a sleeve, matching the raw edges and the seams. Sew the cuff to the sleeve.

WS of the sleeve.

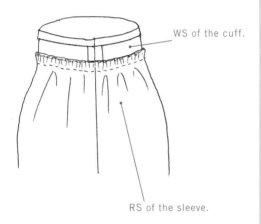

WS of the cuff.

RS of the sleeve.

11 Turn the sleeve right side out and pull the cuff up out of the end of the sleeve.

12 Fold the pressed edge of the cuff over the end of the sleeve to cover the existing stitching, then topstitch it in place. Repeat to sew the other cuff to the other sleeve.

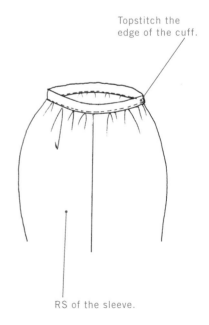

Topstitch the edge of the cuff.

RS of the sleeve.

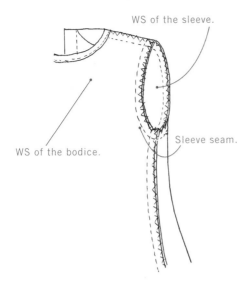

WS of the sleeve.

WS of the bodice.

Sleeve seam.

13 Right sides together, slip the sleeves into the armholes. Sew the seams, neaten the seam allowances, and press them toward the sleeve.

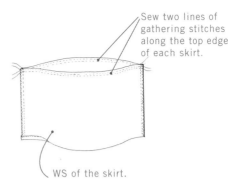

Sew two lines of gathering stitches along the top edge of each skirt.

WS of the skirt.

14 Right sides together, sew the skirts together at the short ends. Neaten the seam allowances and press them toward the back. Press under a ⅜" (1 cm) then a ⅝" (1.5 cm) hem around the bottom of the skirt but do not sew it in place. Gather (see page 139 for technique) the top edge of the skirt and pull the gathers up so that the edge matches the lower edge of the bodice.

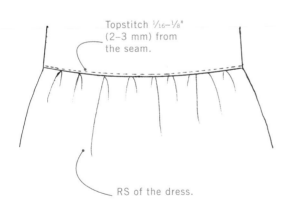

Topstitch ¹⁄₁₆–⅛" (2–3 mm) from the seam.

RS of the dress.

15 Right sides together, pin the gathered edge of the skirt to the lower edge of the bodice. Sew the seam, neaten the seam allowances, and press them toward the bodice, then topstitch them in place.

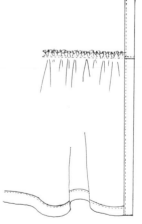

16 Topstitch down one center back hem, around the skirt hem, then up the other center back hem. Make buttonholes in the placket as marked on pattern. Sew buttons onto the button flap to align with the buttonholes.

Puff-sleeved dress

FABRIC
Lightweight wool jersey, 64½ x 30:32¾:35¾:38¼"
  (164 x 76:83:91:97 cm)

OTHER MATERIALS
Lightweight fusible interfacing, 10¼ x 8¼" (26 x 21 cm)
Bias binding ¾" (2 cm) wide, 8¼" (21 cm)
Bias binding 1" (2.5 cm) wide, 27½" (70 cm)

TECHNIQUES
Gathering (page 139).
Binding a center back opening (page 136).
Attaching facings (page 138).
Slip stitch (page 141).

PATTERN PIECES
See pattern sheets A and F.
All pieces cut on straight grain unless otherwise specified.
Seam allowances are ⅜" (1 cm) unless otherwise stated.
Sample is size 3 (see page 142).
The front and back neck facings are shared with the
  Striped Dress (see page 62).

PATTERN PIECES IN BOOK POCKET
1 Front bodice: cut 1 on the fold from fabric
2 Back bodice: cut 1 on the fold from fabric
3 Upper sleeve: cut 2 from fabric
4 Lower sleeve: cut 2 from fabric

5 Front neck facing: cut 1 from fabric + 1 interfacing
6 Back neck facing: cut 2 from fabric + 2 interfacing

PATTERN PIECES TO BE MEASURED OUT
7 Upper skirt: 20¼:21:21½:21¾ x 4¾:5¼:6:6½"
  (51.5:53:54.5:55 x 12:13.5:15:16.5 cm),
  cut 2 on the fold from fabric
8 Lower skirt: 28:28¾:30¼:31½ x 8¼:9:10:10½"
  (71:73:77:80 x 21:23:25:27 cm), cut 2 on the fold
  from fabric

FABRIC LAYOUT

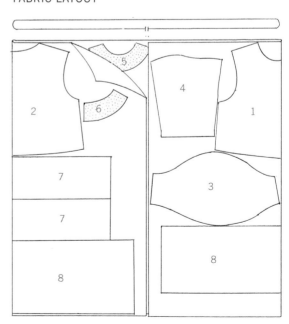

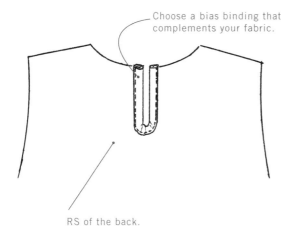

Choose a bias binding that complements your fabric.

RS of the back.

1 Cut open the top of the center back as marked on the pattern. Using ¾" (2 cm) bias binding, bind the center back opening (see page 136 for technique).

RS of the back.

WS of the front.

2 Right sides together, sew the front and back bodice together at the shoulder seams. Neaten the seam allowances and press them toward the back.

3 Iron the interfacing pieces onto the wrong side of all the neck facings. Sew the shoulder seams and press them open. Neaten the lower edge of the facing.

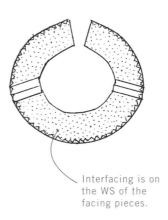

Interfacing is on the WS of the facing pieces.

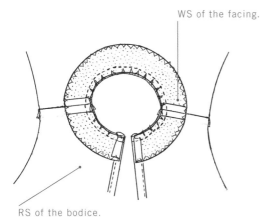

WS of the facing.

RS of the bodice.

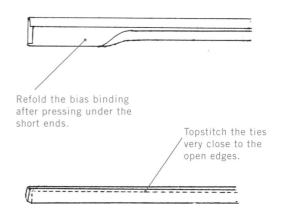

Refold the bias binding after pressing under the short ends.

Topstitch the ties very close to the open edges.

4 Right sides together, pin the neck facing to the bodice neck, matching the raw edges. Fold under the short ends of the facing to align with the edges of the center back opening. Sew the facing in place and turn it to the wrong side (see page 138 for technique), but do not topstitch the edges.

5 Cut the 1" (2.5 cm) bias binding into two lengths. Press them in half lengthwise, then open them flat and press under $\frac{3}{16}$" (0.5 cm) at one short end. Refold and press the lengthwise folds. Topstitch all the open folded edges of both ties.

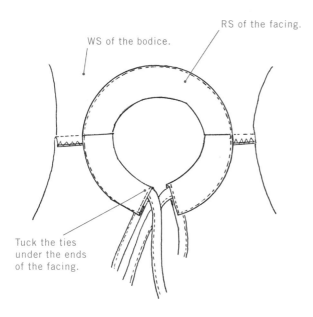

RS of the facing.

WS of the bodice.

Tuck the ties under the ends of the facing.

6 Tuck the raw end of a tie under the facing, so that it protrudes at the top of the center back, as shown, and pin in place. Pin the other tie under the other side of the facing, making sure the two line up. Topstitch across the short end of the facing to the outer edge—catching in the end of the first tie—then around the edge of the facing, then across the other short end—catching in the other tie.

RS of the back.

WS of the front.

7 Right sides together, sew the front and back bodices together at the side seams. Neaten the seam allowances and press them toward the back.

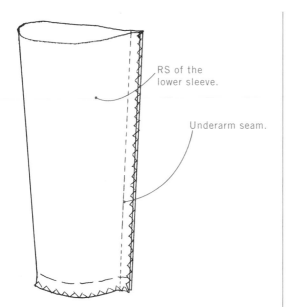

RS of the lower sleeve.

Underarm seam.

8 Neaten the bottom edge of both lower sleeves, then press under a ⅝" (1.5 cm) hem. Unfold the hem and sew the underarm seams. Neaten the seam allowances and press them toward the back.

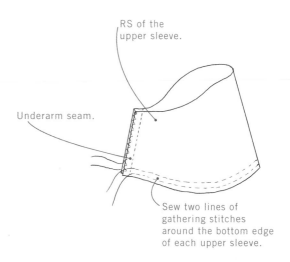

RS of the upper sleeve.

Underarm seam.

Sew two lines of gathering stitches around the bottom edge of each upper sleeve.

9 Gather (see page 139 for technique) the bottom edges of both upper sleeves between the notches. Sew the underarm seams. Neaten the seam allowances and press them toward the back.

10 Pull up the gathers to fit the top edge of the lower sleeve. Right sides together, slip a lower sleeve inside an upper sleeve through the armhole, matching the bottom edge of the upper sleeve and the top edge of the lower sleeve. Sew the seam, then neaten the seam allowances and press them upward. Repeat to make up the other sleeve.

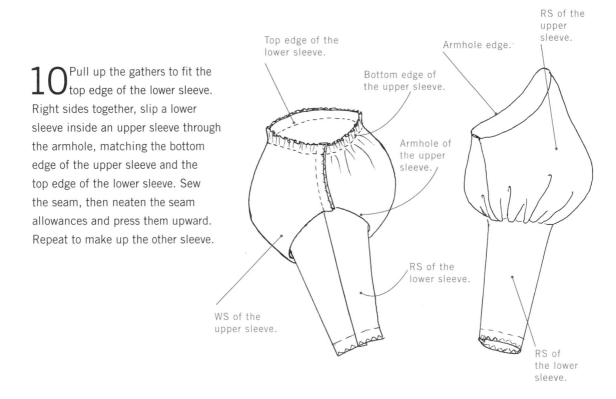

Top edge of the lower sleeve.

Bottom edge of the upper sleeve.

RS of the upper sleeve.

Armhole edge.

Armhole of the upper sleeve.

RS of the lower sleeve.

WS of the upper sleeve.

RS of the lower sleeve.

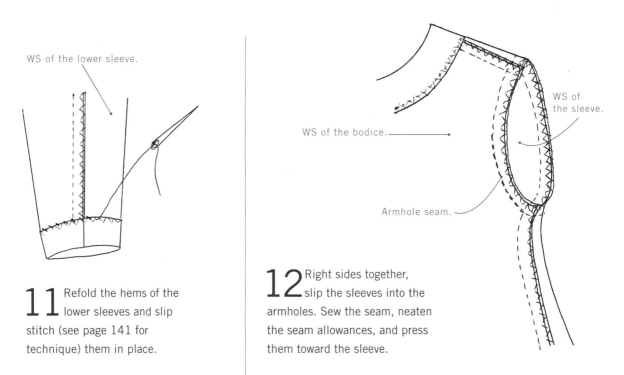

WS of the lower sleeve.

11 Refold the hems of the lower sleeves and slip stitch (see page 141 for technique) them in place.

RS of the upper sleeve.

WS of the sleeve.

WS of the bodice.

Armhole seam.

12 Right sides together, slip the sleeves into the armholes. Sew the seam, neaten the seam allowances, and press them toward the sleeve.

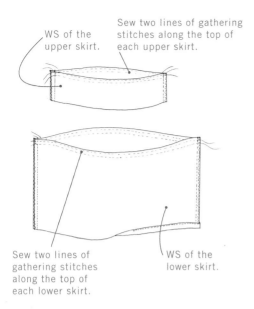

WS of the upper skirt.

Sew two lines of gathering stitches along the top of each upper skirt.

Sew two lines of gathering stitches along the top of each lower skirt.

WS of the lower skirt.

14 Pull up the gathers around the top of the lower skirt to fit the bottom edge of the upper skirt. Right sides together and matching the side seams, pin the gathered edge of the lower skirt to the bottom edge of the upper skirt and sew the seam. Neaten the seam allowances and press them upward, then topstitch them in place.

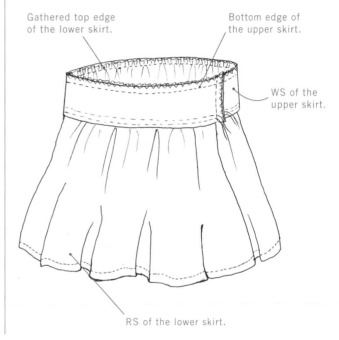

Gathered top edge of the lower skirt.

Bottom edge of the upper skirt.

WS of the upper skirt.

RS of the lower skirt.

13 Right sides together, sew the upper skirts together at the short ends. Neaten the seam allowances and press them toward the back. Gather (see page 139 for technique) the top edge of the upper skirt. Repeat with the two lower skirts. Press under a ⅜" (1 cm) then a ⅝" (1.5 cm) hem around the bottom edge of the lower skirt, then sew in place.

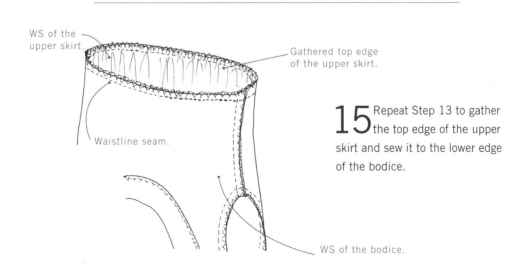

WS of the upper skirt.

Gathered top edge of the upper skirt.

Waistline seam.

15 Repeat Step 13 to gather the top edge of the upper skirt and sew it to the lower edge of the bodice.

WS of the bodice.

Boy's raglan jacket

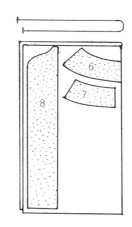

FABRIC

Wool tweed, 61 x 29½:32:34¾:37½"
   (155 x 75:81:88:95 cm)
Lightweight wool, 12⅜ x 18:19¾:21⅛:22½"
   (31.5 x 46:50:53.5:57 cm)

OTHER MATERIALS

Fusible interfacing, 12⅜ x 18:19¾:21⅛:22½"
   (31.5 x 46:50:53.5:57 cm)
Buttons ⅞" (2.2 cm) diameter, 4

TECHNIQUES

Slip stitch (page 141).
Making a patch pocket (page 139).

PATTERN PIECES

See pattern sheets D, I and J.
All pieces cut on straight grain
   unless otherwise specified.
Seam allowances are ⅜"
   (1 cm) unless otherwise
stated.
Sample is size 2 (see page
   142).
The pocket is shared with
   the Unisex Jacket
   (see page 104).

PATTERN PIECES IN BOOK POCKET

1 Back: cut 1 on the fold from tweed
2 Front: cut 2 from tweed
3 Back sleeve: cut 2 from tweed
4 Front sleeve: cut 2 from tweed
5 Pocket: cut 2 from tweed
6 Back neck facing: cut 1 on the fold from wool
   + 1 interfacing
7 Front neck facing: cut 2 from wool + 2 interfacing
8 Center front facing: cut 2 from wool + 2 interfacing

PATTERN PIECES TO BE MEASURED OUT

None

FABRIC LAYOUT

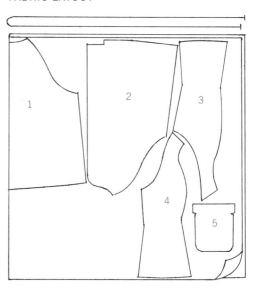

1 Iron the interfacing pieces onto the wrong side of the center front facings. Neaten the long straight edge of the facing.

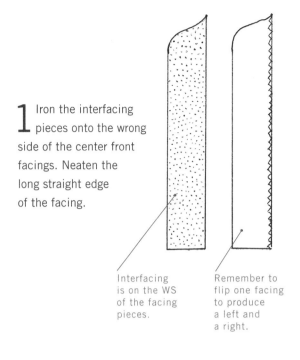

Interfacing is on the WS of the facing pieces.

Remember to flip one facing to produce a left and a right.

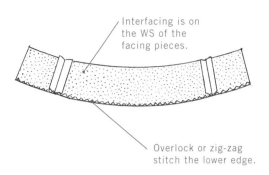

Interfacing is on the WS of the facing pieces.

Overlock or zig-zag stitch the lower edge.

2 Iron the interfacing pieces onto the wrong side of all the neck facings. Sew the shoulder seams and press them open. Neaten the lower edge of the facing.

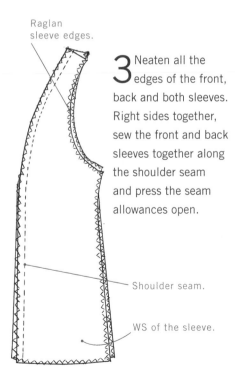

Raglan sleeve edges.

3 Neaten all the edges of the front, back and both sleeves. Right sides together, sew the front and back sleeves together along the shoulder seam and press the seam allowances open.

Shoulder seam.

WS of the sleeve.

4 Right sides together, sew the fronts, sleeves, and back together along all the raglan sleeve seams. Press the seam allowances open.

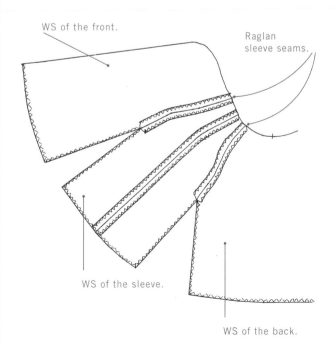

WS of the front.

Raglan sleeve seams.

WS of the sleeve.

WS of the back.

5 Right sides together, sew the center front facing to the neck facing. Make a clip in the center front facing seam allowance at the bottom edge of the neck facing, as shown. Press the seam allowances open.

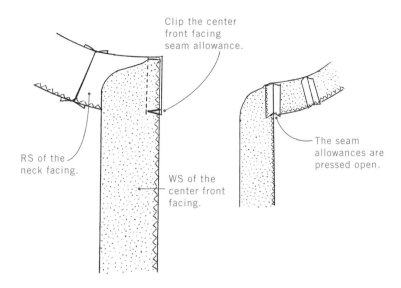

Clip the center front facing seam allowance.

RS of the neck facing.

WS of the center front facing.

The seam allowances are pressed open.

6 Right sides together, pin the whole facing to the jacket, matching the neck and center front edges. Sew across the bottom of one center front, then up the center front and around the neck, then down the other center front and across the bottom of it. Clip the curves and cut off the corner of the lower edge of the center front.

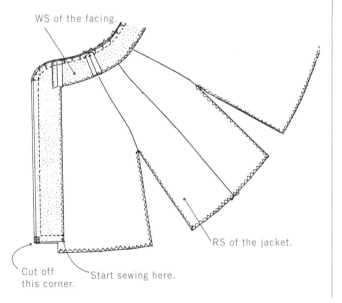

WS of the facing.

RS of the jacket.

Cut off this corner.

Start sewing here.

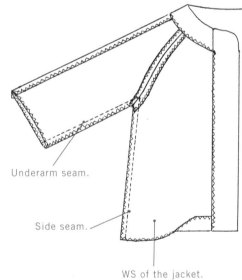

Underarm seam.

Side seam.

WS of the jacket.

7 Press under a 1" (2.5 cm) hem around the lower edge of the sleeves and the bottom of the jacket. Unfold the hems and sew the underarm and side seams from wrist to bottom edge. Press the seam allowances open.

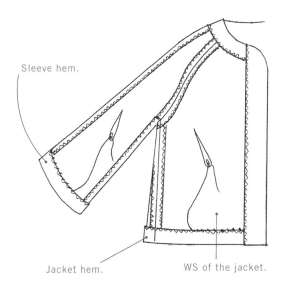

Sleeve hem.

Jacket hem.

WS of the jacket.

8 Refold the hems and slip stitch (see page 141 for technique) them in place.

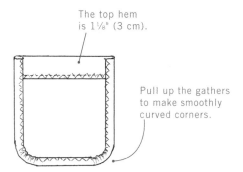

The top hem is 1⅛" (3 cm).

Pull up the gathers to make smoothly curved corners.

9 Make up both patch pockets (see page 139 for technique). Press under a 1⅛" (3 cm) hem across the top of each pocket and sew it in place. Sew the pockets onto the front of the jacket as marked on the pattern.

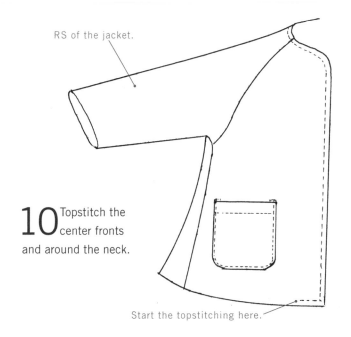

RS of the jacket.

10 Topstitch the center fronts and around the neck.

Start the topstitching here.

11 Make buttonholes in one center front as marked on the pattern. Sew buttons onto the other center front to align with the buttonholes.

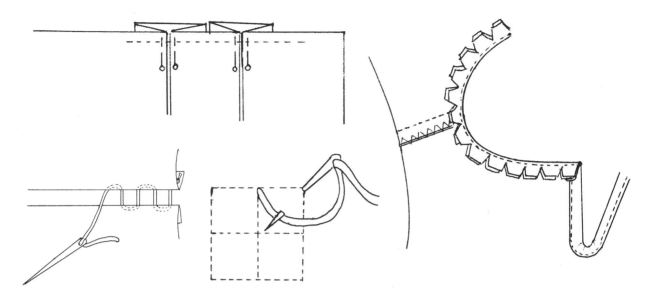

techniques

MOST OF THE PROJECTS IN THIS BOOK REQUIRE
ONLY FAIRLY SIMPLE SEWING SKILLS, BUT
THERE ARE A FEW TECHNIQUES THAT YOU
MAY NOT HAVE TRIED BEFORE, AND THE
INSTRUCTIONS FOR THOSE ARE GIVEN HERE.
IF SOMETHING IS COMPLETELY NEW TO YOU,
THEN YOU MAY WANT TO PRACTICE IT ON SCRAP
FABRIC BEFORE WORKING ON YOUR PROJECT.

Binding an armhole

Whether you are binding an armhole with purchased bias binding or a bias-cut strip of fabric, the technique is the same.

1 If you are using a bias-cut strip of fabric, then prepare it first. Fold the strip in half lengthwise and press the fold. Open the strip out flat and press one raw edge in to lie along the first pressed fold.

2 Right sides together and matching the raw edges, pin the flat edge of the binding to the armhole, easing it around the curves. Sew the binding in place, taking a 3/16" (0.5 cm) seam allowance, and reversing at each end to secure the stitches. Using the tips of the scissors, snip little notches into the seam allowance around the curved sections.

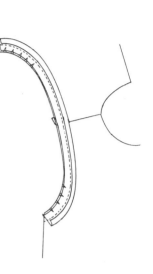

3 Fold the binding up over the raw edges and press it, pressing the seam flat. On the wrong side, press the seam allowances toward the main fabric. Make sure that the folded edge of the binding is pressed neatly flat along its length.

4 Fold the binding to the wrong side and pin it in place, smoothing and easing the curves. Topstitch the folded edge in place, sewing 1/16" (1–2 mm) in from the edge.

Binding a center back opening

If you are using a strip of bias-cut fabric, then prepare it as for Binding an Armhole (see page 135).

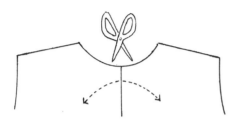

1 Cut along the center back marking on the pattern, cutting carefully and accurately to the bottom of the line.

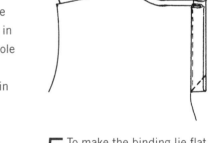

2 Open out the cut edges completely, so that they run in a straight line as shown. Right sides together and matching the raw edges, pin the flat edge of the binding to the center back opening. Sew the binding in place, taking a ³⁄₁₆" (0.5 cm) seam allowance, and reversing at each end to secure the stitches.

3 Bring the opened-out edges back together and, using the tips of the scissors, snip little notches into the seam allowance around the curved bottom of the opening.

4 Press the binding over the raw edge and topstitch it in place as for Binding an Armhole (see page 135): you'll find it easiest to open it out flat again to do this.

5 To make the binding lie flat around the bottom of the opening, push it through to the wrong side and sew a short diagonal line across the bottom of the curved section, as shown. Reverse at each end to secure the stitches. Press the little flap to one side so that the binding forms a neat, flat V on the right side.

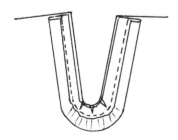

Making box pleats

You need to make these pleats neatly and accurately for a professional-looking finish.

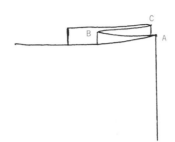

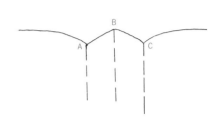

1 The pattern piece is marked where each pleat needs to be made: there are three marks, labelled here as A, B and C.

2 Fold the fabric wrong sides together at A and C, and right sides together at B, to make a triple fold as shown.

3 Press along 1³⁄₁₆–1⅝" (3–4 cm) of the the fold lines at A and C firmly, and the line at B lightly.

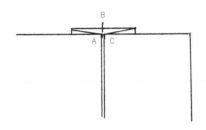

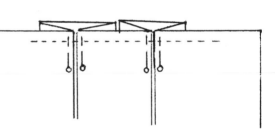

4 Fold in A and C to meet on top of B, matching all the pressed lines.

5 Pin each pleat close to A and C. When all the pleats are made, sew across the tops of them to hold them in place, sewing ⁵⁄₁₆" (0.8 cm) from the raw edge and being careful to keep everything lying flat. In this illustration the pleats are shown as slightly three-dimensional so that you can see how they are formed, but once you have sewn across them they will lie flat.

Attaching facings

These create a very neat finish, but you do need to sew accurately for the best result.

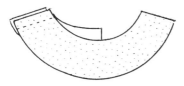

1 Matching them carefully, iron the neck facing interfacing pieces onto the wrong side of all the neck facing fabric pieces. Taking a ⅝" (1.5 cm) seam allowance, sew the shoulder seams and press them open.

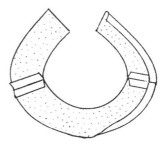

2 Turn under and press a ⅜" (1 cm) hem along the lower edge of the facing, easing the hem to lie flat around the curves.

3 Right sides together and matching the raw edges, pin the facing to the neckline. If the facing is being sewn to a neckline that has a bound center back opening (see page 136), then you will need to press under a ⅜" (1 cm) hem along each short straight edge of the facing, as shown here. Do this before pressing under the lower edge hem. Match these short straight folded edges to the bound edges of the opening. Taking a ⅝" (1.5 cm) seam allowance, sew the facing in place. Using the tips of the scissors, snip little notches into the seam allowance around the curved sections.

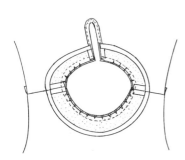

4 Press the notched seam allowances toward the wrong side of the garment, making sure that the stitching line is just visible on the wrong side, as shown.

5 Turn the whole facing to the wrong side, easing it flat around the neckline and ensuring that the seam is rolled to the wrong side. Pin the lower edge in place, then topstitch close to the edge.

Gathering

This is the best way to produce even gathers along the edge of a long piece of fabric. If a particular section of a piece is to be gathered, it will be marked on the pattern with notches.

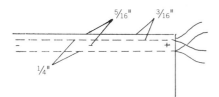

1 Loosen the tension on the sewing machine and set a long stitch length. Along the edge to be gathered, sew two straight lines of stitches. Sew one line ³⁄₁₆" (0.5 cm) in from the raw edge, and the second line ¼" (0.7 cm) below the first line; that is, ½" (1.2 cm) in from the raw edge. Do not reverse to secure the stitches, and leave long tails of thread at the end of each line of sewing. Reset the sewing machine for normal sewing.

2 Right sides together, pin both ends of the piece to be gathered to the flat piece it is to be attached to. Find the mid-point of each piece and pin those together, too. Then, starting at one end, pull on the tails of thread to gather up the fabric. Pull gently and slide the gathers along evenly as you go. When you have gathered one half to fit the flat piece, gather the other half starting at the other end.

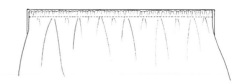

3 Pin the two layers together, making sure that the gathers are even. Taking a ⅝" (1.5 cm) seam allowance, sew the layers together.

Making a patch pocket

These are simple, practical additions to a garment. You'll need a piece of thin, stiff cardboard to help shape the curved edge.

1 Neaten the edges of the pocket piece by overlocking or zig-zag stitching it. Press under a double hem the depth given in the project instructions across the straight top edge and sew it in place.

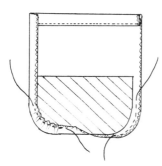

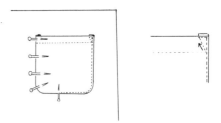

2 Press under ⅜" (1 cm) around all raw edges of each pocket piece. To make flat, neatly curved bottom corners, first run a row of gathering stitches (see page 139) around the corner, within the seam allowance. Using the paper pattern piece as a template, cut a piece of thin card to the shape of the curve. Lay this card on the fabric, ⅜" (1 cm) in from the edge, and pull up the gathers around it. Then press the hem carefully, making sure the curves stay smooth.

3 Pin the pocket piece to the garment in the position marked on the pattern. Topstitch it in place around the edges, leaving the top, straight edge open. To reinforce the top corners, sew little triangles of stitches, as shown.

Ladder stitch

This is used to sew up a gap in a seam.

1 Thread the sewing needle and knot one end of the thread. From the wrong side, take the needle through the folded edge of one piece of fabric, hiding the knot in the seam allowance. Make a small stitch through the folded edge of the other piece of fabric. Then make a small stitch through the folded edge of the first piece, making sure the thread runs straight across the gap between the two pieces, as shown.

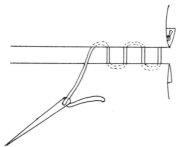

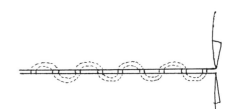

2 Pull up the stitches as you sew to invisibly close the gap.

Slip stitch

This stitch is used to almost invisibly sew a hem in place. Pin the hem in place before sewing it.

1 Starting at the right-hand end of the hem, bring the thread out from inside the hem, just below the folded edge. Make a tiny stitch into the fabric above the hem and about ⅜" (1 cm) along from where the thread came out. Pick up just a couple of threads of the fabric in this tiny stitch—it should be almost invisible on the right side.

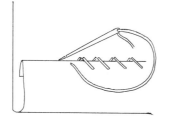

2 Make a diagonal stitch down into the hem, to come out in line with the first stitch through the hem. Continue in this way to sew the whole hem in place.

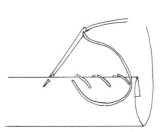

Feather stitch

This is a simple embroidery stitch you can use to decorate the yoke of the Girl's Shirt (see page 70). If you prefer, you can draw chalk lines on the fabric as guides, but feather stitch doesn't need to be perfectly evenly spaced to be charming.

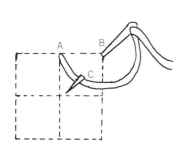

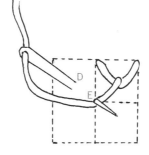

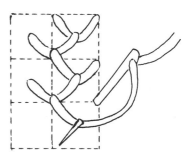

1 Make a straight stitch from A to B. Bring the needle out at C, midway between and below A and B. Make sure the loop of thread lies under the point of the needle.

2 Pull the thread through and gently taut. Make a stitch to the left, going in at D and coming out at E, as shown. Again, make sure the loop of thread lies under the point of the needle.

3 Continue in this way, working alternate stitches to the right then to the left.

Pattern sizes

The paper patterns are graded by size rather than by a child's age, so measure the child you are sewing for and choose a pattern size using the chart below.

In the project instructions, the different quantities of fabric needed for each size, and the measured pieces for each size, are separated by colons.

	SIZE 1	SIZE 2	SIZE 3	SIZE 4
Height	39½" (100 cm)	43¼" (110 cm)	47¼" (120 cm)	51" (130 cm)
Chest	21¼" (54 cm)	23" (58 cm)	24½" (62 cm)	26" (66 cm)
Waist	19½" (49 cm)	20" (51 cm)	21" (53 cm)	21¾" (55 cm)
Hip	22½" (57 cm)	24" (61 cm)	25½" (65 cm)	27½" (70 cm)

Pattern legend

The markings used on the patterns are given here.

····························	Size 1
– – – – – – – – – –	Size 2
— – — – — – —	Size 3
———————	Size 4
⟷	Straight grain of the fabric
⤢⤡	Cross grain of the fabric (cut on the bias)
⇧⇧	Cut on the fold
⊤	Notch
⊏⊐	Pocket position
····	Horizontal buttonhole
⌐	Vertical buttonhole
+	Button

Fabric layout for Round-Collared Dress (page 118).

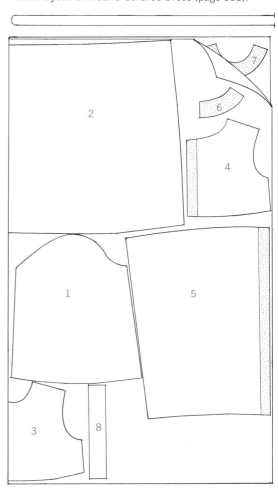

Resources

Mariko Nakamura makes a range of garments
for sale, including the styles in this book.
Visit www.aquarela.co.uk for more information.

Fabrics and haberdashery used in this book
came from:

Liberty
www.liberty.co.uk

The Cloth Shop
www.theclothshop.net

The Cloth House
www.clothhouse.com

Lyndons Stitch & Beads
197 Portobello Road
London W11 2ED, United Kingdom
Tel: 020 7727 4357

Acknowledgments

I dedicate this book to my mother, Akiko, and to
the memory of my father, Hiroshi, who passed
away during the making of it.

I would like to send a very special thanks to my
children, Lirio and Mateo. This book is a kind of
sewing diary, as the pictures were taken during
holidays and weekends out with them and my
husband, Pedro, who took all the photographs.

Thank you very much to Kate Haxell, Elizabeth
Healey, and Amy Christian, for their invaluable
work in the writing, design and production of
this book.

First published in the United States in 2015 by

Interweave
A division of F+W Media, Inc.
4868 Innovation Drive
Fort Collins, CO 80525
interweave.com

Library of Congress Cataloging-in-Publication Data
Nakamura, Mariko.
  Stitch, wear, play : 20 charming patterns for boys
& girls / Mariko Nakamura
  pages cm
  Includes index.

ISBN 978-1-63250-140-0

1. Children's clothing. 2. Sewing. I. Title.
TT635.N35 2015
646.4'06--dc23

                                    2014037463

10 9 8 7 6 5 4 3 2 1

Manufactured in China by 1010.

INDEX